Devotions *to* Nourish
Your Body *and* Soul

A *Woman's*
Path to
Inner Beauty

Author of *Beauty Secrets of the Bible*
Ginger Garrett

HARVEST HOUSE PUBLISHERS

EUGENE, OREGON

Author photo © Don Sparks Photography, Atlanta, GA, www.DonSparksPhotography.com

Cover photo © Fancy Photography / Veer

Cover by e210 Design, Eagan, Minnesota

Some devotions were adapted from Ginger Garrett's blog, www.GingerGarrett.com.

Harvest House Publishers has made every effort to trace the ownership of all poems and quotes. In the event of a question arising from the use of a poem or quote, we regret any error made and will be pleased to make the necessary correction in future editions of this book.

Published in association with MacGregor Literary, Portland, Oregon

A WOMAN'S PATH TO INNER BEAUTY
Copyright © 2011 by Ginger Garrett
Published by Harvest House Publishers
Eugene, Oregon 97402
www.harvesthousepublishers.com

ISBN 978-0-7369-3000-0

Printed in China

11 12 13 14 15 16 17 18 / RDS-NI / 10 9 8 7 6 5 4 3 2 1 *

To every woman who longs for
true and lasting beauty.

Acknowledgements

I'd like to thank the Harvest House publishing team for welcoming me into their family and making this book such a joy to work on. May all your efforts to serve the Lord and bless readers be returned tenfold into your lives! I owe a special thanks to Delta Airlines for cancelling a flight due to bad weather, which left me stranded in an airport with Jean Christen of the Harvest House team. Jean and I met for the first time that day on the concourse and discovered we had much in common, including a heart for women's issues. And to LaRae Weikert for sifting through all my ideas and keeping an open door when inspiration strikes—thank you! And finally, for Barbara Gordon, an editor with such a gentle and gracious touch. Thank you!

I also owe a debt of gratitude to the readers who have sent me emails over the past two years since *Beauty Secrets of the Bible* was published. You shared experiences, insights, and encouragements. I pray for you all so often. May God bless you and lead you deeper into His grace and peace.

A Note to You from Ginger

*W*elcome! Within these pages you'll find words of comfort and inspiration and a challenge to open your heart to the truest meaning of beauty. It's my prayer that you'll treasure the scriptures I've selected, and that God will use this little book to do a great work in your life and in the lives of the women around you.

Let me begin with the certain truth that you are beautiful. Does that surprise you? You may not feel beautiful. You may feel run down, overwhelmed, frumpy, overweight, wrinkled, past your prime, or any number of adjectives we've invented to describe ourselves. But let me assure you: You are beautiful! And it's okay to feel beautiful. Feeling beautiful is really about feeling free, and freedom comes from knowing the truth. And real truth is based on God's Word and His love for you.

As we walk together through these pages, I am praying for you to find God's perfect freedom in beauty. You can become…

- free to love others more fully and accept their love more completely in return

- free of depressing habits and oppressive thoughts
- free to accept yourself and others unconditionally

Are you ready to start our journey? We're going to discover the beauty that is unique to each of us and uniquely God's—a beauty you and I are called to give away. We'll be discovering what God says about beauty and your purpose in this world.

All His great blessings to you,

Ginger

Finding Hope

*Hope deferred makes the heart sick,
but a longing fulfilled is a tree of life.*

PROVERBS 13:12

At a certain age, a woman must choose between her face and her hips." I don't know who said this, but as women we experience peer pressure about our appearance almost our entire lives. When we're young, fat is our nemesis. As we age, fat keeps our faces looking youthful. At some point, as this saying suggests, we have to decide if we're going to be fashionably thin or fashionably young.

This never-ending battle or circular question brings us right back around and deposits us at the beginning. I notice the lines on my hands, so I slather on hand cream faithfully every night. Then I notice that my neck needs dire attention. I run out to buy firming cream for my neck, and the saleslady gently suggests I may want to "invest" in a firming cream for my thighs first. Meanwhile, I'm off to the gym every day to build lean muscle, burn fat, and hope my swimsuit is kind to me this year. Once I was worried I wouldn't fill out my swimsuit; now I'm worried I'll fill it out in all the wrong places.

This much is clear: At every stage in life the worldly

definitions of beauty will be right beside us, whispering in our ears that we need to try harder. Beauty, by the world's definition, will always be just beyond our grasp. Worldly beauty is a "hope deferred" because we can't catch it, grasp it, or claim it. And the Bible warns that hope deferred will make our hearts sick.

As you pray through your body issues, ask God to reveal to you where your hope truly lies. Ask Him to guide you as you journey through these pages so that your hope will be set on the right things and your heart will be strengthened and healed.

Lord, I pray for what You alone can deliver. Fulfill my longings as I seek You. Please free my heart, revolutionize my definition of beauty, and change my future forever so I can honor You in everything I do.

Honoring Others

Honor one another above yourselves.
ROMANS 12:10

ow you catch a man is how you have to keep him."
I was single and on the prowl for a good man when
these words from an older woman caught me off-guard. *She's
right,* I realized. *If I'm spending all my time on my appearance,
trying to catch a guy by being beautiful, I'll catch a guy who
only wants a beautiful gal. And that won't be a problem...until
I start to fall apart.* Even in my tender twenties I knew there
was an expiration date on my looks. However, when I married, I wanted it to last forever. Clearly this older woman
knew something I didn't.

Around this same time, I met a man who had married a
lovely girl. This lovely girl gained an enormous amount of
weight after the wedding. "I wouldn't mind the weight," he
confided to his friends, "if only she treated me with respect."
He was in pain because she treated him in an ungodly manner. He was willing to trade having a lovely wife for having
a loving wife.

Here is a secret God taught me as I began to live a life
grounded in Scripture instead of *Cosmo* magazine: Men may

like to feel good about the women on their arms, but it's more important that the women on their arms make them feel good about themselves.

God's Word tells us to focus our considerable energies not on our appearance, but on our actions. God wants us to consider how we honor and serve others. He wants us to spend more time pruning rather than preening—cutting off unkind words, selfish thoughts, and greedy habits. He wants us to communicate love, respect, honor, and doting affection to the men in our lives. Whether you're looking to catch a man or keep one, beauty begins in the heart.

> *Lord, the world emphasizes appearance yet You emphasize action. Show me where I have placed the greater emphasis in my life. Help me love others, give respect and affection, and communicate Your acceptance and encouragement. Make my true beauty— my life in You—radiate to the hurting souls around me. Open my heart and help me love.*

Healing Your Past

*Ask and you will receive, and
your joy will be complete.*

JOHN 16:24

Whose good opinion do you most want to win? Who can say the words you believe will heal your heart? For some of us, we long to hear our fathers' voices telling us we are beautiful. For others, they want to hear from boyfriends or husbands. For some it may be men we've been in relationships with. Maybe we wish we could go back to high school and walk the halls, winning the approving stares of all the girls who made fun of us.

As long as we continue to imagine that their opinions have power to heal, we won't listen carefully for God's voice—the true voice of healing. Yes, we can choose to live in the past, but the past is dead. The wounds may still be festering, but those days are gone. The people have moved on or even died. We've been left alone to suffer. There is no way to return to those old moments for healing. Let me state this message plainly: My sister, the one who wounded you cannot heal you.

So what are you to do with your wounds? I believe your wounds are invitations for miracles. These sores persist by the grace of God to bring you a deeper healing than you ever thought possible. Your hurts remain because they need a supernatural salve. God loves to tend to His daughters. He wants to heal your wounds. He is a God of lavish love, outrageous miracles, amazing gifts, and fathomless affection. Praise God your wounds exist. Praise Him that He did not allow healing through ordinary means, that you were not healed in a ho-hum way. Praise Him for the miracles He is going to do because you brought your whole self, wounds and all, to the foot of the cross. Praise God that He doesn't want you to hide your wounds, thinking them too small, or petty, or old to be healed.

Lord, I wait for You and Your healing touch. I give You all of me today—my past, my present, my future. Heal my wounds, bind up my broken heart, and show me Your miraculous love. Send me to those who also need Your healing love so I can point them to You.

Learning to Laugh

A cheerful heart is good medicine.

PROVERBS 17:22

Just a few weeks after delivering my third baby, I went out for my first post-baby run. I bundled up in extra layers because the winter winds were especially cold. I burst out the door, relishing the freedom of running alone. A man on a motorcycle passed by and gave me a thumbs-up sign. *Amazing!* I thought. *I may be postpartum, but I guess I'm still attractive!* The man on the motorcycle slowed down and circled back. Now I started to panic. This guy might be a creep. As he approached me, he held out a business card. "I really admire people like you," he said. I looked at the card. He was a weight-loss coach.

Around this same time, I had an elderly neighbor who seemed to be suffering from dementia. One day she waved at me as I walked past. I stopped and she said, "You look good, considering…" At this, she lost her train of thought and never finished the sentence. I still wonder what she was going to say.

Sometimes what really needs to lighten up is *me,* and I'm not talking about my weight. I love those two meetings I just shared because they remind me that I can't take myself or the battle of the bulge too seriously. It's life after all. And while there may be a thousand weight-loss supplements on the market, no medicine is as good for me as laughter and good cheer. Joy turns mountains into molehills. Good cheer energizes the spirit. Laughter refreshes the weary heart.

Whatever you're facing today, I pray you find the humor that underpins each day. I hope you will give yourself permission to laugh and make merry.

Lord, I need a good laugh today. And if it comes at my own expense, maybe that's even better. Help my heart to be light, even as I face serious struggles and setbacks. Remind me today of the many reasons I can be of good cheer and see the delight woven into the world around me.

Finding God in the Darkness

*The earth was formless and empty, darkness
was over the surface of the deep, and the
Spirit of God was hovering over the waters.*

GENESIS 1:2

How did Da Vinci paint mesmerizing women such as the Mona Lisa? By controlling light and shadow he focused the viewer's eye. Shadow is as important to the masterpiece as light. But only because Leonardo was a master, and in his hands darkness and shadow became tools. Light is made brighter, the finished product more stunning because of the presence of shadows and darkness.

When you think of darkness, what usually comes to mind? I'm sure it's a negative association or emotion. But what if I told you that God, as the Master artist, utilizes shadow and darkness? Indeed, Scripture tells us that God is at work in the darkness and indwells those places our human eyes can't see. Darkness in Scripture seems to have two associations: the darkness of spirit, when God and Jesus are rejected, and the darkness of God, which is His playground. Let's talk specifically about the second type of darkness—the darkness God blesses through His presence. According to Genesis 1:2, life began in darkness. God was in the darkness, preparing an astonishing creation. "God said, 'Let there be light,' and there was light" (Genesis 1:3).

As humans, we naturally fear darkness. We fear what lurks in the night. We fear the loss of goodness and hope. But in truth, God uses darkness to create, to call forth new life, to astonish us with His creative passion.

Do you fear you've lost your way and are stumbling in the dark? Do you worry that God won't find you? Dear one, God is not afraid of any darkness! He can use it to call forth new life and new works. Do not give up on yourself or become dismayed by the blackness. Trust in God and His marvelous, creative passion and steadfast love for you.

Lord, I sometimes feel so lost—like a child in the dark. I am afraid I've lost my way. But my true safety is in You. Do something extraordinary in my life, Master, using the shadows to point to Your dazzling light.

Finding Counsel

Your statutes are my delight;
they are my counselors.

PSALM 119:24

Who gives you counsel? Who do you turn to for learning about beauty? There are many beauty "experts" in the world. Most offer knowledge, And knowledge, correctly applied, is wonderful. Wisdom, however, is life-saving. Wisdom about beauty and its implications in our lives will sustain us long after our looks have faded. True wisdom feeds our spirits, our hearts, and our bodies. It allows us to have what others only chase: the deep security of being forever loved and accepted and the radiant glow of peace.

Spending time in God's Word is where we find wisdom. As we delve into Scripture, its truths become our counselor. And counselors have a knack for getting to the root of an issue, don't they? A great counselor can expose hidden motivations and offer life-affirming solutions. God's Word can be that counselor for you if you spend time reading and meditating on it regularly.

I've always said that every hunger is an invitation for God to reveal Himself. The hunger for beauty is an invitation to discover God's love for us and around us. Your hunger for beauty has led you to this book, and I pray this book will stir a desire to get into God's Word more often. As you do, you'll receive wise counsel that delights your soul and sets you free to soar. And what is beauty but true, radiant freedom?

Lord, You are marvelous! I wanted to be healed and set free of my anxieties about beauty, and I find that You offer that plus so much more. You desire to give me an abundant life, filled to the brim with goodness and mercy. Thank You for inviting me to drink from Your cup of life and wisdom.

Exercising the Truth

I run in the path of your commands, for you have set my heart free...I will walk about in freedom, for I have sought out your precepts.

PSALM 119:32,45

What's your favorite way to exercise? (Please tell me you have one!) Do you have a scripture verse or passage you meditate on while you move? Today's two verses are some of my favorites. I love to run and walk, and these verses fill me with joy as I do. They also help me focus on why I exercise.

Why do you exercise? What goes on in your head while you're active? Do you scold yourself about foods you've eaten, the number on the scale, the wiggle in your thighs? While you're exercising, are you imagining a sleeker self, someone who is the envy of everyone on the beach when you parade around in a bikini?

When exercise becomes punishment or strictly the means to a better body, it loses some of its benefit potential. Exercise is for the inner woman as much as it is for the outer shell. Studies confirm that exercise causes chemical changes in the brain and body that uplift mood, chase away depression and anxiety, foster clear thinking and creativity, and build physical stamina for everyday living. And when exercise is paired with outdoor settings and friends, these effects multiply.

I encourage you to make exercise a celebration of freedom. Listen carefully to your inner dialogue the next time you exercise and if you need to, make some positive changes.

Lord, I've been taught that exercise is the key to a slim figure, and the world worships thin. But exercise is also meant for so much more. Use my exercise time to speak to me, to help me foster relationships, and to bless my mood and body. Thank You for everything You do through my exercise.

Freedom from Shame

May your unfailing love come to me, O LORD,
your salvation according to your promise;
then I will answer the one who taunts me,
for I trust in your word.

PSALM 119:41-42

How do you answer taunts about your appearance, your weight, your life? Whether the taunts come from memories of mean people, cruel neighbors, children, or even from your own "inner critic," you can respond appropriately by deciding what to do in advance.

Psalm 119:41-42 tells us the best way to handle ugly voices of condemnation: We are to remember *where we stand* and *where we are going.* We answer taunts by standing firm in the security of being unfailingly loved and the certainty that God's Word is true. The Bible promises us blessings, peace, acceptance, love, and eternal freedom. Taunts may seem like attacks only on us, but they are also attacks on God and His plan for our lives. Taunts whisper that we've failed, we're too fat or thin, too plain or too fussy, too imperfect to be worth loving. Malicious teasing encourages us to run away from the love and acceptance found at the foot of the cross.

Negative words and comments make fun of us as we bow our heads to our Creator and thank Him for His plan for our lives, including our bodies and our longing for beauty.

Heeding taunts will drive you away from love. Listening to God and accepting His Word will always highlight His love for you. Today, if someone taunts you, be ready to answer with the certainty of God's unfailing love and salvation. You need to be reminded of it, and the person teasing you needs to hear it.

Lord, taunts hurt when I was younger, and they hurt today even though they're not always so obvious. People can be so cruel to each other, and I'm sometimes cruel to myself. Protect my heart and spirit. Cleanse me of evil thoughts toward others and myself. I want to be an encourager instead of someone who tears down people. Help me become a woman who makes the world a kinder place in Your name.

God's Creative Spirit

Stop and consider God's wonders.

Job 37:14

I shopped for wigs today. "Just for fun," I promised my nervous husband. I perused a rainbow of colors: platinum blondes, fiery reds, smoky browns. And then I moved on to makeup. If I changed my hair color, I'd need new makeup to complement the look. *And maybe new clothes,* I rationalized. Give me a mall, a Visa, and one hour, and I can give you a completely different me.

Is there any other creation of the Lord's that is so wildly changeable? Can you think of any animal or plant that can boast so many looks, so many alterations in appearance? Have you ever stopped to consider that while God's Word sets many standards, He never sets one for our actual appearance. (He does speak of modesty and godliness.) He doesn't tell us what color to keep our hair or which side to part it on. He doesn't tell us if He prefers us to wear frosted eye shadows or mattes, comfortable sneakers or high heels, whether He prefers blue eyes or green. He doesn't even set standard weights or minimum height requirements. God loves variety, and most of the women I know do too.

We are creative spirits born as creatures made by our loving Creator. The heart of innovation flourishes best and brightest where there is no shame, where creativity is an expression of joy and playfulness, and where we are honored and appreciated. As we dress for each day, how we present ourselves is a unique exercise that reflects our individuality. We express our love for simplicity, for peace, for passion, for color, and for flare. Our creative joy is a gift of our heavenly Father!

Lord, thank You for making me a woman. Thank You for the unique ways I express my heart. I'm so glad You love me just as I am and allow me the freedom to play with my appearance so long as I keep my focus on honoring You. Awaken the creative desires in my spirit and remind me they are from You.

Influence or Attention?

*This day I call heaven and earth
as witnesses against you
that I have set before you life and death,
blessings and curses.
Now choose life, so that you and
your children may live.*

DEUTERONOMY 30:19

Which do you prefer: attention or influence? We can usually look at how a woman or girl is dressed and tell immediately. Some of us dress for attention. We want to tell the world we are beautiful women with breasts or legs or midriffs. Attention feels good to hungry hearts, and we feel admired and loved. If people are staring and smiling, they must like us, right? Especially men. When a man stares, it must mean we are desirable, correct?

Unfortunately no. I'm reminded of a story about my great-grandmother Mimi. When she moved into a retirement home, an elderly Casanova pursued her daily. He was notorious for having relationships with lonely widows. One day Mimi exited her room and Casanova broke into a serenade when he saw her.

"Listen," Mimi snapped, wagging her finger at him, "I haven't got one little bit left." She turned and stomped off.

Mimi was done with attention. She had influence, and she much preferred that. Everyone loved her and delighted in her company. I was in my teens and Mimi in her eighties, but her opinion mattered more to me than any rock star or popular peer's thoughts. Mimi had the power to change people's lives through what she said because she emphasized the wisdom she garnered through life. May we all become women whose words are remembered far longer than our beauty.

Lord, this world places much of my worth on my appearance. Garnering attention matters to the world far more than gaining influence. Getting attention feels good for a few minutes, but gaining influence has the power to change lives for You forever. Help me prioritize between the two and to clearly spot opportunities to tell people about You.

Living for Today

This is the day the LORD has made;
let us rejoice and be glad in it.

PSALM 118:24

God has not made tomorrow yet. He has not made "someday," "when I," or "after that." God made today. So often, especially when thinking of beauty issues, we live more for tomorrow or the "when I's": "When I lose this weight…"; "When I have more money…"; "When I…I'll be happier."

What will it take for you to rejoice and be glad for today? If you're like me, you'd need a dash of acceptance to rejoice today in who you are. You'd need a dollop of humility to be glad for today even though you and your life are not perfect. And you'd need a sprinkling of peace to let go of tomorrow and live right now.

So often today's scripture verse is considered only a children's song—a sweet and innocent song little ones clap along to on Sunday mornings. In reality, Psalm 118:24 is a profound challenge, a call to live in the purest peace. And it's the secret to living in radical freedom.

You've been given today. This moment is the sum total of

your choices. Rejoice! There is no stone God can't move out of your way today, no mountain that permanently impedes your progress. There is only His presence, this hour, and your willing heart.

Lord, thank You for today. Show me how to live abundantly in each moment, each hour, each day. When I lay my head on my pillow tonight, I want my heart to be full of the knowledge that You were with me every step I took—guiding me, correcting me, nurturing me.

Beautiful Worship

> *Not to us, O LORD, not to us but to your name*
> *be the glory, because of your love and faithfulness.*
>
> PSALM 115:1

We live in a culture of glory and worship. The problem is we're worshipping each other and giving glory to mortals. The Internet, arguably the most powerful social tool in history, seems to be used mostly to track celebrities, look at pornography, and focus on ourselves through blogs and social Websites. One popular singer has more than 1500 discussion groups about her—and that is just at one site! People make good livings stalking the famous for pictures of them leaving the gym, getting coffee, or other mundane activities. When we support companies that shell out millions to look at a celebrity's baby photo while children are dying all over the world for lack of essentials such as clean water, our priorities are terribly wrong. Our passion for worship isn't the problem—our focus is.

We need to turn away from shallow pursuits and standards of beauty that don't originate with God. The intense worship we give people diminishes what we offer to God. And when we don't wholly worship God alone, we also miss blessings because we are distracted by our interests in photos or news reports of someone we will probably never meet.

Let's choose to be diligent about our hearts so we won't be swept into emptiness and alienation. We seem to believe that focusing on celebrities and self-interest offer us reprieves from our wounds and might fill our hungry hearts, but they won't. We were made for love—but it's a special love based on the only Person who can meet our needs. We were made to worship, but we need to discipline our focus to God alone.

> *Lord, I feel like I'm walking in a minefield. Everywhere I look celebrities or news about them clamor for my attention. It's easy to fall into the trap of believing that fame or beauty or wealth will bring me love and influence. But I know that's not true. Please remind me that my worth is in You. Lead me into Your truth. I pray the words of Psalm 27:11: "Teach me your way, O LORD; lead me in a straight path."*

True Beauty

*Your beauty should not come from outward
adornment, such as braided hair and the
wearing of gold jewelry and fine clothes.*

1 Peter 3:3

The Bible doesn't say we can't wear jewelry, makeup,
or fancy clothes. But it does say adornments should
not be the *source* of our beauty. God wants His daughters
to have the best, and when we're talking about beauty, His
heart remains true to His principles. God wants you to have
authentic beauty. The world offers plastic rhinestones; God
offers perfect diamonds. Our heavenly Father doesn't want
us to settle. He wants to give us loving gifts that last forever.

True beauty comes from inner radiance, deep peace, and
a loving spirit. These qualities are what people so desperately
need to see in us, experience from us, and be taught by us
how to achieve them.

Can inner qualities really be "seen"? Can our spirits make
us more beautiful to others? Absolutely. In several scientific
studies volunteers were asked to rate the beauty of strangers in photos. Some strangers were frowning and scowling. Others had smiling, pleasant expressions. Consistently

volunteers rated those who smiled as more attractive. We all react positively to people who project a positive attitude.

Authentic beauty is centered around serving others. When we express love, acceptance, and affirmation, others see us as more attractive than the sum of our physical parts. Our inner light radiates beauty and calls them to us to discover our secret, which is Christ Jesus living within us.

Lord, I want the beauty You advocate and provide. Authentic beauty springs up within me through Your Spirit and casts light to a lost world. Help me shine before others so when they look to me I can point them to You.

Suffering

*He has not despised or disdained the suffering
of the afflicted one; he has not hidden his face
from him but has listened to his cry for help.*

PSALM 22:24

One day after dealing with a painful health condition for months, I was in the shower scrubbing up and spouting off. I was angry that I was suffering. It was disrupting my plans and interfering with my life. Then the voice of the Holy Spirit came to my heart. He said, "Suffering is not unusual. Suffering is the normal state of this world."

I stopped and thought about that. Time passes and we grow old. Bodies age, wrinkles form, and eyes dull. That is the normal state of this world. Aging is a form of suffering we experience as we go through the inevitable decline and decay that always ends in the death of our physical bodies. Our hearts recoil at the thought—at the horror—of our mortality. That's because death was never intended to be a "normal" state for us. We were created as eternal beings, and we were meant to live forever with God. But because of sin, our bodies now die. That is humanity's "new" normal brought about by sin. Yes, our bodies will fall apart and quit. It's depressing, but it's the truth.

There's no sense, then, in trying to cling to what will be lost. Why place so much emphasis on bodies we can't keep to an ideal standard and looks we can't maintain? When we adopt a proper perspective, we discover that true beauty is timeless. It transcends appearance and triumphs over the ravages of time.

And the blessing? There is no expiration date on this beauty! We can't lose it, and it won't fade away with the years. Some women (and men) may choose to spend thousands in the doctor's office trying to hold on to their youth, but we know that spending time in the presence of our loving God does more for our faces and bodies than any scalpel, syringe, or cosmetic regime.

Authentic beauty does more than just endure—it becomes more radiant with the passing of time. Because of Jesus, our spirits live forever and enhance every aspect of who we are. Beauty can once again be our normal.

Lord, with each passing day I am closer to being with You. With each loss comes a great promise, and in one of the greatest losses for humans (death) You offer the promise of eternal life. I choose to believe in You. Thank You for loving me and supporting me in all the seasons of life. Please turn my sadness into joy as Your light shines through me to reveal the beauty of Your love.

Respecting God's Work

*The fear of the LORD is the beginning of
wisdom; all who follow his precepts have good
understanding. To him belongs eternal praise.*

Psalm 111:10

As we learn to respect God's handiwork in our bodies
without constant criticism and condemnation, we
push open the doors to the prison of shame we were in. Freedom from shame about our looks, our weight, and every aspect
of our bodies begins with our deepening respect for God.

Self-criticism places us on the throne of our lives because
we're basically saying we believe and value our judgments
over God's. Our dissatisfaction with who we are and how
He built us hails our standards as the benchmark. This rel-
egates God's wisdom and principles to obscurity. But when
we made the decision to trust, respect, and even fear God, we
also made the decision to believe in His choices. We affirmed
His creation as beautiful and in good taste. We proclaimed
to the world and to our hurting hearts that God's many ideas
about beauty are to be cherished. We uphold the truth that
each of us is a unique expression of His handiwork.

Self-criticism and condemnation are not just attacks on

ourselves. They also attack God. As you meditate on God's power, His creation, His majesty, you will grow in respect and fear of Almighty God, Creator of the heavens, the earth, and you. This "fear," which I define as a unique combination of awe and respect, leads to wisdom. And wisdom is the companion of all beautiful women because it teaches us to see ourselves and others in the light of Jesus and the truth of eternity with Him. When we view the world through this lens, nothing looks the same.

The more you respect—deeply revere the Lord and His artistry—the more wisdom will take root and grow in your life, leading to even more freedom and growth as you become a deeper expression of God's divine beauty.

Lord, I have stubborn, self-critical opinions about my body, my appearance, and my worth. I've made decisions along life's path to trust my judgment over Yours. Forgive me. Help me develop a deeper awe and respect for You.

Labeling

*Know that the LORD is God. It is he
who made us, and we are his; we are
his people, the sheep of his pasture.*

PSALM 100:3

*L*abels are judgments, and judgments usually tend to
carry the aura of legitimate authority. Are you aware
of the labels you've accepted? They often reveal who or what
you recognize as trustworthy sources and resources. When it
comes to looks, labels are everywhere and insidious.

Consider the label "figure flaw," which is often applied to
parts of a woman's body she's not pleased with. Who said the
shape or condition of the feature in question is a flaw? Flaw
implies a mistake by the designer. So if you accept and promote the label (and concept) of "figure flaw" for an area of
your body, you are accepting or agreeing with the notion that
God made a mistake when creating you. And that means
you're saying that God is flawed.

Remember, fashions change but God never does. One generation prizes curvy, plump women; another worships lean,
athletic types. Different cultures vary within each generation
as well. Humans have so many standards that, ultimately, no

standards apply. What is considered a figure flaw in New York might be considered your best asset in Madrid. The next time you're tempted to label yourself or others, remember your words reveal who you trust most. Labels tell your heart who to follow.

Speaking of labels, have you considered that God has labels for you? His labels for you include: "His," "beloved," "delightful," "beautiful," "wholly accepted," and "deeply loved." You are His creation, His daughter, a sheep belonging to the Great Shepherd.

Lord, it's so easy to buy into labels, even the negative ones. Open my eyes to see what labels I've embraced and help me toss them aside if they're negative. Show me the labels I give to other people that aren't life-building and help me change. Thank You for labeling me as Your beloved daughter.

Freedom from Fear

*Whoever listens to me will live in safety and
be at ease, without fear of harm.*

PROVERBS 1:33

My youngest daughter tries to get into bed with my husband and me at least one night a week. She has bad dreams, and on those nights she doesn't feel safe unless she's sandwiched between us. She can't sleep until she's there, and once she's there, we can't sleep at all. But there's no negotiating with a child who feels scared. She can't be forced to accept the truth. She's too afraid, and what she feels is infinitely more real, more important at that moment than what is actually true. Reality is no match for undisciplined imagination.

I confess there are moments when I'm no different than a frightened child. My feelings are too strong for the truth to break through. All I can do, it seems, is patiently wait out the storm of emotion until my heart is ready to listen to the truth and act on it. Can you relate? So often we don't feel beautiful, and those feelings are so strong that we're unable to accept the truth. We're frightened about life, about love, about our futures. We are convinced that we're not good enough, thin enough, or pretty enough. We fear that we'll never get control of our eating or that we'll never achieve the standard of perfection we want.

There's no better place to run to in those moments than God's presence. Fix a cup of hot tea, open the Scriptures, and curl up in God's wisdom. The storm of emotion will pass, and God's love will penetrate your heartaches and fears. Sometimes we need to be comforted and reassured before we can take in the truth. God's Word can ease your turmoil, and He will keep you safe in the storm. You never have to be ashamed or slow in running to the comfort of your heavenly Father's arms.

Lord, some days there is such a frenzy of emotion within me that I can't concentrate on Your truth. On those days, comfort me. Wrap Your arms around me and reassure me of Your love through Your Word.

Acceptance

Accept one another, then, just as Christ
accepted you, in order to bring praise to God.

ROMANS 15:7

 have a dear friend who once was depressed over her
weight and the constant sense of rejection she felt.
Everywhere she went she felt people's disapproving stares and
condemnation. They didn't care about who she truly was,
she felt. They only cared about the number on the scale. She
didn't fit the cultural standard, and so she was being judged
harshly.

My friend lost the weight...and her sense of rejection
deepened. People gave her no notice. She fit the standard
now, and yet they largely ignored her. They approved of
her, she could tell, but that was what hurt so much. They
approved of her weight but not her. They didn't know her,
care about her, or have any interest in her. All that mattered
was her appearance.

When we act to win the acceptance of others, we discover
that our wounded hearts and spirits can't be healed by people. They can't give us the medicine we need. They can give
us acceptance and approval, but eventually we realize these

aren't enough to heal our wounds. The pain was inflicted by people, but only God can heal them. No amount of physical perfection can heal our hearts. And changing our appearance to find happiness and hope is like rearranging the deck chairs on the *Titanic*. A good effort, perhaps, but completely futile.

If your heart needs healing, go to the healer of hearts! Allow Jesus to do what you can't do for yourself. He has told you that you, a daughter of God, are accepted, beloved, and precious in His sight. God will never love you more than He does right now because He loves you perfectly! Everything is all right, dear one. You are all right, and you are dearly loved.

> *Lord, help my emotions line up with the truths in Your Word and Your heart. When I am longing for acceptance and receive rejection from people, comfort me with the knowledge that I am loved more deeply, more wonderfully, more abundantly by You than I can imagine.*

Beautiful Scars

Accept one another, then, just as Christ
accepted you, in order to bring praise to God.

ROMANS 15:7

*Y*ou know how deep the pain of rejection can go. The poison spreads in your spirit, souring relationships and spoiling life. Rejection says you aren't worthy, don't measure up, can't be loved as you are. Some of us tried to overcome taunts by fixing what we thought was broken— our bodies, our faces, our clothes. But this pursuit was "snake oil" medicine that cured nothing and cost us dearly.

Praise God that we are not the women we used to be. Because God in His mercy brought us through those trials and is still delivering us from bondages today, we have something real to offer a hurting world. We know the medicine that heals!.

We have something to offer the people around us. We bear the scars of feeling unloved and unlovely, but they can show others that there's hope. Remember the apostle Thomas? He didn't believe Jesus rose from the dead until he saw with his own eyes and Jesus spoke to him personally. Jesus said, "Put your finger here; see *my* hands. Reach out your hand and put it into *my* side. Stop doubting and believe." And then Thomas believed.

We don't know whether Thomas actually touched Jesus' scars, but we know the scars were a testimony to Thomas of God's mind-blowing power.

Friend, there is a woman out there who needs to see your scars. She needs to know others have been wounded just as she is and God delivered them with His loving grace and mercy, raising them from a world of pain into a beautiful new life. I encourage you to be open about what you have suffered. Let God use your scars to draw others to you and, ultimately, to Him.

Lord, it's tempting to hide my past pain and failures. But in You there is no shame. Use my scars to remind women of Your grace and mercy. Help me show them that You are the solution to the pain they feel.

A WOMAN'S PATH TO INNER BEAUTY

Your Inner Dialogue

*May my meditation be pleasing to him,
as I rejoice in the LORD.*

PSALM 104:34

challenge you to consciously listen to your inner dialogue for a day. What goes through your mind when you look in the mirror? When does your "inner critic" scream the loudest? At the grocery store, at church, at the pool? What triggers set off a flurry of criticisms?

Now, think back. Where did you first hear voices and words like these? Who taught you to criticize yourself? And most important, why did you internalize their views and make them your own?

Our fallen natures take in messages of shame and anger, and then we often spend years trying to mask them, compensate for them, change them, or eliminate them. We'll work harder, try harder, and strive to win our freedom by our own efforts. We attempt to conquer our inner "demons" by correcting what they believe. But inner demons don't want to listen or release us.

We become prisoners of our inner critics, paralyzed by the fears of failure and rejection. Some women may choose to hide their appearance under baggy clothes or lack of grooming, hoping that if no one notices them, the inner voices won't be awakened. Others attempt to be so impeccably perfect that the inner critic shouldn't be able to find fault with anything they do, wear, say, or weigh. Unfortunately this doesn't work.

One powerful answer to evicting your inner critic is to read God's Word. Today's verse, Psalm 104:34, is especially potent. Does the writer give us any clue as to what his inner dialogue sounds like? Yes! The writer is rejoicing in God. We too can choose to rejoice or criticize, but we can't do both wholeheartedly at the same time. Rejoicing in the Lord can drown out the negative voices and give you relief from the debilitating rejection you feel when they snap at you.

Lord, help me turn my thoughts to rejoicing over You instead of finding fault with me. May my meditations be pleasing in Your sight. Help me in this battle because I don't want to give one more minute of my time to a false, lying internal dialog. Comfort me and build me up so I can experience Your joy.

Promises

*Your kingdom is an everlasting kingdom,
and your dominion endures through all
generations. The LORD is faithful to all his
promises and loving toward all he has made.*

PSALM 145:13

A promise made by God is a promise kept. His Word is absolute and completely dependable. Contrast that to the empty promises that drive profits in the beauty industry. If all the promises for wrinkle creams were true and each one took ten years off my face, I would look like a Girl Scout right now. Promises mean profits—not performance—when it comes to advertising. In fact, promises in the beauty industry are one-sided. They mean good things for the companies and very little for the consumers. Did you know cosmetics are seldom regulated by the FDA? That means beauty industries promise to "minimize pores" or "combat cellulite" but they often don't have the research or facts to back up their claims. The promises are made to *entice* you not to guarantee specific results.

Women worldwide spend billions every year on beauty products. Yet a recent survey found that only two percent of

American women consider themselves beautiful. Promises lure us to spend, but the majority of women won't get the satisfaction or results they hope for. That's because beauty is ultimately a feeling, not a physical state. Beauty is feeling loved and loveable, desired and wanted. No product can make us beautiful despite promises to the contrary.

One of the many blessings of having a loving God is that His promises are kept. God promises us that we will thrive under His care and have everything we need. He will do for us what the worldly concept of beauty cannot. And best yet, God's promises are for everyone. We only need to believe in Him and the salvation He offers through His Son, Jesus Christ. What God promises, He delivers.

Lord, thank You for the reassurance You give me in Your Word. It overflows with Your love, Your promises, and Your provision. I know that true beauty transforms from the inside out, and this is the beauty You provide. Because I am created and loved by You, I am beautiful.

Defining Beauty

*Do not conform any longer to the
pattern of this world, but be transformed
by the renewing of your mind.*

ROMANS 12:2

eauty impacts our well-being every day. Today's culture prizes women's beauty above their intellect, above their dreams, above their contributions to family, community, and society at large. The message to women is clear: If you're not beautiful (according to the world's definition), you're not of much worth or relevance.

Thank God we have a very different, more accurate concept of worth and relevance! In fact, as revealed in today's verse, we have direct orders from God to avoid conforming to the world's expectations, to resist its demands, and to rise above its empty lures. Right now I'm sitting in front of a window with a delightful view of a Bradford pear tree. Two brightly colored blue jays are fussing at each other, fighting for dominance. Ironic, isn't it, that the prettiest birds in my garden are also the most quarrelsome? I could set out enough birdseed to feed them until they burst, but that's not enough. They want dominance over each other. Top billing in the animal world equals security and a promise of getting needs met.

But we're not animals on the bird scale. We're *daughters* of God living in an animal-like arena, where dominance over others is sought and worshipped. Beauty, its pursuit and worship, is a form of dominance over others.

God commands us to renew our minds, which happens as we dwell on the truths found in His Word and agree with them in our hearts. We need to hear truth, read truth, and speak truth. God put our eyes, ears, and mouths right next to our brains. The way to our minds is through those three facilities. And when our minds are renewed with truth, we're able to do something truly amazing: know God's perfect and pleasing will for our lives—in this world and for eternity.

> Lord, I'm beginning to understand that the world wants me to conform to its ideas of beauty because so much of my heart is at stake. I don't want dominance over others; I want an indwelling of Your truth and Your Spirit. What others chase without hope, You give me freely. Thank You.

Beauty in Freedom

I will walk about in freedom,
for I have sought out your precepts.

PSALM 119:45

An elephant trainer was once interviewed about his technique. A visitor to the training pen was awed as he watched adult elephants held in place by ropes they could easily break. Why didn't the elephants try to escape?

The technique was quite simple, the trainer explained. When the elephants were babies he began training them. He tied a strong rope around one of their legs to keep them standing in place in the ring. As babies, he said, the rope was enough to hold them in place, and the elephants learned they couldn't break free. As the beasts grew, so did their strength. They could easily snap the ropes now, but they didn't because their minds had accepted that the rope was stronger than their muscles. Their minds held them captive—not the physical rope.

So often what we perceive as truth when we are young is not the truth at all, but we haven't revisited it as we've grown in wisdom. We internalize messages about ourselves and our appearance. We grow up and change but the internal messages don't. We call ourselves the same names we were called as a child. We think we're weighted down by the same ropes, when in reality we've been able to break free for years.

To be free and to feel beautiful may simply mean finding the willingness one more time to break away from the tethers that tied us up as children. You've grown and you've changed. You've accepted God's offer of salvation and chosen to follow and believe Him. Those old ropes can't hold you anymore!

Lord, You have set me free. I'm ready to break loose from the flimsy ropes of old lies. Help me break the strands that hold me back and become the woman You created me to be. Give me Your vision for my future. I know freedom in You awaits!

Feeling Beautiful

If it is possible, as far as it depends on you,
live at peace with everyone.

Romans 12:18

When we see another woman, our first response is often to compare ourselves to her. And usually we're on the losing end of the equation. She might have better hair, longer legs, whiter teeth, or a thinner body. We silently berate ourselves for falling short…again.

The danger in comparing ourselves is not only emotional, but it has a physical danger too. If we don't have and maintain deep connections with other women, if we aren't able to be authentic with them, we shorten our lifespan. As my friend Shelley Hendrix says, we become competitors instead of companions.

But if we can live as companions, there are unexpected rewards. One study proved that women with deep friendships with other women cut their risk of early death by more than 60 percent.[1]

God designed women to need other women. Without each other, we wither. Without each other, we die too young. Staying connected feeds our spirits, which gives us the will to live and take care of ourselves mentally, emotionally, and physically. So learning to break the comparison habit will increase our beautiful feelings and alter the course of our lives for the better. In fact, it can even alter the course of our sphere of influence and the world around us.

Lord, help me stop comparing myself to other women. I want You to work fully in this area of my life so I can live in true community with others. I want to know companionship and blessing instead of competition and envy. May other women sense the difference in me and be drawn to Your love shining through me.

What Does She Need?

*Each one should use whatever gift he
has received to serve others, faithfully
administering God's grace in its various forms.*

1 PETER 4:10

When I experienced a devastating season of infertility, I eventually noticed that I had a constant refrain running through my brain whenever I saw a family. Like a scrolling headline on a TV news channel, I had one sentence going around my mind at all times: "Look what she has that I don't!" I was eaten up with jealousy and bitterness. God had given other women the very things I wanted: beauty, babies, and wealth.

And I wasn't just jealous. I was also angry. Furious, in fact. God said He loved me, but He gave what I most wanted to someone else. To my hurting heart, God was either lying or callous. At times I thought I couldn't bear the pain. But I did one thing right: I kept reading my Bible and soaking in God's truths. I read devotionals and spiritual messages. I forced myself to stay near to the God I thought had hurt me. One day evidence of God's incredible healing burst forth. When I saw another woman who had what I wanted, a new thought surged through my mind: *What does she need that I have?*

When I asked that question, my life was transformed. My relationships with other women, with God, and with myself changed forever. I learned that I may not have everything I want, but I have something someone else needs. I am here not to get, but to give. Someone may be more beautiful, thinner, wealthier, and blessed with a huge family, but I have been given something that person needs. I am here to minister God's grace to her.

I encourage you to practice the art of lovingkindness to other women—even the women who seem to have everything you need and want. Live in peace by letting go of comparisons. A woman at peace with herself and at peace with other women is powerful. She has a beauty that can't be bought or taken away. Her beauty transcends appearances. It feeds her spirit, her friendships, and her future.

Lord, may I be a woman who serves, not seeks. Help me look at other women as companions, not competitors. Help me remember that I have been given something rare and special that others need. Grant me the privilege of sharing Your grace with them.

Laughing at Ourselves

*You know my folly, O God;
my guilt is not hidden from you.*

PSALM 69:5

rowing up in Texas, I loved how plain-spoken our ministers were. One youth minister, when teaching us about modesty, put it this way: "If it ain't for sale, don't advertise it." I've never forgotten that lesson even though I know I've made some bad fashion purchases that revealed way too much. The only way to salvage those purchases was to layer on other clothing and hope no one ever noticed. But the truth always has a way of, shall I say, exposing itself?

A while back I took my daughter's Girl Scout troop camping. As usual I was rushing to get everything packed. I threw in a pair of khaki pants so low-cut across the midriff that my entire stomach was revealed. I planned on wearing a big fleece shirt that fell all the way to my thighs. No one would ever see the immodest waistline.

I took the girls for a long nature walk to a beautiful campsite overlooking a lake. As I leaned down, my shirt fell forward and exposed my ample behind as the pants' waistband gaped open in back. At this moment, a hapless wasp flew toward the blinding white light of my "moon." I jerked upright, trapping him between my cheeks. He panicked; I panicked. He stung; I squeezed and slapped.

In the bathroom as I nursed my wounds he fell to the floor, dead and as flat as a pancake. I had no less than six stings in a place where I dared not ask any ranger to render aid. So, ladies, remember: Immodest clothes are never appropriate. And sometimes, just sometimes, you might hear God laughing when you slip up and try to get by.

Lord, You sure have a great sense of humor. Help me laugh at my foibles. I don't want to take life so seriously that I miss Your sense of delight. Sometimes it's better to laugh about my mistakes than to cry over them. Give me a light heart as I walk in Your truths today.

No More Self-criticism

Since this is the kind of life we have chosen, the life of the Spirit, let us make sure that we... work out its implications in every detail of our lives. That means we will not compare ourselves with each other as if one of us were better and another worse...Each of us is an original.

GALATIANS 5:25-26 MSG

One major key to letting go of critical self-talk is to understand the connection between faith and the comparison game. When we compare ourselves to another woman, we are really asking, "Who do You love more, God, her or me?" If we judge ourselves as "less than" the other woman in any capacity, we're accusing God of not loving us enough to create us as well as He created her. Think of it this way, if your children made a list of all the Christmas gifts they wanted, and you bought those gifts but passed them out to other children, how would your children feel? Unloved. Angry. Unwilling to trust you.

When we decide another woman got what we really wanted (that skin! that body! that man!), we erode our faith in a loving God. We decide God does not see or, even worse, does not care about us. And we decide He can't be trusted.

But the truth is that beauty isn't about looking a certain way or getting what we want. It isn't about winning love and acceptance from others. Beauty is about the power of attraction—the power to attract others to God through His light within us. The wonderful drawing power of joy, contentment, excitement, and satisfaction. Of showing off our God who always says, "You are loved and accepted." (Yes, even when we sin His love doesn't stop. But His heart is grieved until we repent and turn to Him for forgiveness and mercy.)

We want to be beautiful so we will be accepted and loved. God made us just as we are—loved—so others would seek Him and His love too. But for that equation to work, we have to be willing to trust that God gave us the right gifts, the right form, the right design to communicate Him to hurting sisters.

Someone today needs you to shine because she's lost. Hold your head up and refuse to be shamed and shut into the darkness. Stay in God's light and draw the woman in.

Lord, forgive me for accusing You of not loving me when I know You really do. Help me let go of critical comparisons and accept myself as You created me. Show me how I can offer this same acceptance to other women. I open my heart to You and wait expectantly.

Beauty in Healing

The tongue has the power of life and death.

PROVERBS 18:21

In the 2009 *Glamour* magazine body image survey of 16,000 women, 95 percent of respondents said getting compliments from other women helps them like their shape.[2] We can play a powerful role in helping our sisters heal and achieve inner peace and acceptance. One way we can do this is by being aware of how often women are criticized and then countering that negativity with encouragement. I challenge you to choose a day this week to look for and notice any negative gossip and criticism targeted at women. Scan the tabloid headlines at the market checkout. Listen to a few minutes of "celebrity news." Check out blogs directed at girls and young women. You'll be shocked as I was, I'm sure, at the viciousness of the attacks regarding the slightest rise in weight or not weighing enough, individuality in fashion choice, and so on.

Beauty is truly a battlefield. While we may be tempted to write most comments off as trivial sales gimmicks, or entertainment, or a world apart from us, the truth is that our spiritual enemy uses appearance as an open door to slap us, needle us, insidiously drag us down, and pollute our minds.

But we are not defenseless! We've got weapons. Words are powerful tools against shame. With your words you can foster healing in a wounded world. I like to compliment women on their beautiful spirits, upbeat attitudes, the colors they wear, or maybe a beautiful piece of jewelry they have on. You have your own way of complimenting others, I'm sure. Each effort to bless another woman is a way to honor God and allow His love to heal hearts and spirits.

Lord, You've given me a unique and powerful ability. With my words I can participate with You in building up people. Help me use my words only for the good of others. May every word I say today be a blessing to someone.

Beauty in Acceptance

I took you from the ends of the earth,
from its farthest corners I called you.
I said, "You are my servant";
I have chosen you and have not rejected you.

ISAIAH 41:9

A n odd trend is happening on fashion runways in New York City and Paris. As popular culture begins to celebrate diversity in women's bodies and sizes, high-fashion models are getting thinner and younger. Some models have caused audible gasps as they've stepped onto the runway because they are so thin they look ill. Why would high fashion reject popular opinion and embrace anorexia as a career choice? Because they, along with the rest of the beauty industry, make money from their exclusivity. If everyone can have it, it's not worth much, is it? The rarer the item, the harder it is to get and the more that can be charged. The more women the industry can exclude, the more special the accepted participants become.

Most of us probably remember this lesson from grade school. Some girls created cliques and excluded other girls, which resulted in hurt feelings. Worldly beauty thrives on exclusion too. Is there a clique you just can't seem to get into?

Maybe the one for women with long, lean legs; or the one for women who have flawless skin; or the one for women who exhibit the ultimate in feminine curves? Are your feelings hurt? Are you frustrated?

Well, here is some crazy news: So are the women in those cliques! Exclusion makes everyone miserable because people know they aren't perfect. Everyone suspects they are unworthy. Seldom does worldly acceptance make a dent in the walls around our hearts, and even in the rare instances it does, the joy never lasts. Hurting women use exclusion as a physical way to express a battle raging inside their hearts. It has nothing to do with you. It is no reflection of your worth.

Lord, I can't control other people's behavior. Even when I know Your truth, when I walk in Your truth, when I accept Your truth, others may seek to shame or ridicule me. I know I am beautiful in You, so this must be an issue between them and You. Reach out and touch them, Lord. Offer them Your healing, Your compassion, Your mercy, Your love.

Miracles Still Happen

You are the God who performs miracles;
you display your power among the peoples.

PSALM 77:14

According to a survey of more than 1000 physicians completed by Health Care Direct Research, the majority of doctors believe miracles can happen.[3] Let's dwell on this for a moment. Doctors are scientists on the front lines who deal with broken lives and hurting people. They encounter depression and disease every day. And yet these doctors are largely convinced miracles can happen. They are convinced because they've probably witnessed them!

Miracles don't happen because people are good or special. They happen because *God* is good. We can't earn a miracle any more than we can earn His grace and forgiveness. In fact, the grittier our battles become, the greater the setting for a miracle. Whatever is dragging you down into the mud today, whispering that you will never recover, never be happy, or never be free of a bad habit or addiction, let me assure you that God can find anyone anywhere and do amazing transformations! Miracles happen every day to ordinary people.

There is hope for you! God has not forgotten you. He

will meet your every need. You can be free from what holds you back. You can know wholeness, forgiveness, and peace. Whether your struggle is—an eating disorder, shame from the past, fear for the future—God is in the business of helping. Don't be afraid to ask for assistance, and don't stop believing that miracles are possible.

Lord, what an encouragement Your grace is to me. I can bring You all my problems and fears, handing them to You to take care of and transform them into miracles that reveal Your loving heart. Remind me often that You are a God of miracles who loves me.

Beautiful Timing

*Go, gather together all the Jews who are
in Susa, and fast for me... When this is
done, I will go to the king, even though it is
against the law. And if I perish, I perish.*

ESTHER 4:15-16

Why do swimmers drown in the ocean when an undercurrent grabs them? Often it's because they immediately attempt to get to land by swimming *against* the current. Experts advise that the smarter strategy is to stay calm and allow the current to sweep you along until you sense it weakening; then, and only then, is it time to fight and swim through it to safety.

Fighting against the current isn't wrong, but your timing can be. Sometimes timing makes all the difference. We see this principle illustrated beautifully by Queen Esther, whose story appears in the Old Testament book of Esther. When learning about the king's edict to massacre her people, Esther didn't rush immediately to her husband and fight or rant and rave. Though she was the most beautiful woman in the land and had great prestige, Esther chose to wait. She prayed and fasted for three days, and even then she didn't fight. She invited the king and his advisor Haman, who was the insti-gator behind the coming massacre, to a banquet. She invited them to a second banquet the next night. Then she acted. By praying and fasting, by waiting, by being wise, Esther saved the Jews.

Now, I doubt you will be swept out to sea today or dis-cover a plot to destroy your people, but you may well be confronted with co-workers obsessed with money and diets, neighbors who want to sweep you into their gossip and crit-icisms, family members who have a few "helpful" things to say about your weight or appearance. Ask God to grant you the wisdom to know what the best approach is and when. Pray and wait for His guidance. God will reveal His perfect timing for your situation.

Lord, sometimes people say or do things that hurt so I react badly. I know the best approach is to pray and wait for Your wisdom. Please give me the will and patience to stop, pray, and wait for Your guidance when I get upset.

Beauty in Sacrifice

*They made the bronze basin and its bronze
stand from the mirrors of the women.*

EXODUS 38:8

After God led His chosen people, the Israelites, out of
bondage in Egypt, the time finally came for them to
build a tabernacle for worshipping God. Today's verse notes
that the women donated their mirrors for its construction
This intrigued me. In the ancient world a mirror was a treasure. Of all the items women could offer to God, why did
they choose their mirrors? I went to a rabbi I know who
explained the situation to me this way:

> Consider how the men were treated while slaves in
> Egypt. They were treated like animals, whipped and
> abused daily. The Jewish women honored their hus-
> bands by making themselves lovely every day before
> their men came home. Without the women saying a
> word, their appearance spoke volumes to their hus-
> bands. Their lovely appearance hinted, "You are hon-
> ored in my sight. You are not an animal. You are a
> man, and I respect and love you."

Can you see the essential character of godly beauty illustrated in this story? Godly beauty is not an objective standard we try to attain that is measured by certain weight goals, hair lengths, and silky smooth skin. Rather, the desired effect of our appearance is to lift others up and honor God. Beauty is about service, about communicating worth and honor to those God has placed in our social circles. Tending to our appearance isn't a measure of our worth; instead, it's a measure of how we value others. Worldly beauty tells us we must be beautiful to be worthy. Biblical beauty tells us that because others have worth, we strive to communicate honor and love.

Lord, root out every selfish and self-centered idea I have about beauty. Give me a fresh vision of beauty according to Your perspective. Show me how I can use everything You've given me to bless and affirm the people I have contact with. May my appearance and demeanor today whisper to my precious loved ones that they are esteemed and adored.

Past or Present?

*Praise the LORD, O my soul, and forget not all
his benefits—who forgives all your sins and heals
all your diseases, who redeems your life from the
pit and crowns you with love and compassion,
who satisfies your desires with good things.*

PSALM 103:2-5

id you get good grades in grammar school? I didn't.
(Which is why God shows me mercy by assigning
great editors to work with me, although what the editors did
to deserve such punishment is beyond me.) But I do know
the difference between past tense and future tense when writing. Future tense is a promise, as in, "You will be given something."

What does grammar have to do with beauty? In the Bible—
everything. I've noticed that Satan likes to speak in the future
tense, promising us we will be given something if we'll only
agree and act on his suggestions. Doesn't this shed a bright
light on our assumptions about beauty? What motivates us to
pursue beauty is often the *promise* that we will be given something, that we will garner love and acceptance. Only if we conform our appearance to "their" standards—lose the weight,

get the hair done, and invest in an up-to-date wardrobe—will we be worth loving. Those promises are conditional based on performance.

God never bases His love for us on our performance or appearance! His great love and mercy, His affection and delight in you are based on who He is, not who you are. Because God is gracious, all His benefits are freely yours: forgiveness, redemption, healing, love, compassion, desires satisfied, and youth renewed. The blessings are the benefits of knowing God and accepting Jesus as Lord and Savior, not the by-products of our own efforts.

Satan says that because of who we are, we can't be loved. God's Word says that because of who we are, we are loved.

Lord, help me see clearly the false promises I've believed. The world promises love, acceptance, and respect if I can look like a model or movie star. That's a lie, Lord. You've already given me love, acceptance, and honor. Help me live in Your truth and walk in Your love.

Making Peace with Food

*When you have eaten and are satisfied, praise the
LORD your God for the good
land he has given you.*

Deuteronomy 8:10

God doesn't want His children to starve. Many of
today's diets restrict calories to such a severe degree
that the plans would qualify as starvation in a Nazi con-
centration camp. (This is not an exaggeration.) Starving prisoners is usually done to break their spirits, rendering them
incapable of fighting back. This sends a chill up my spine;
does it yours?

Dieting to control weight has a long, long history. In the
1920s, diets regimes were devised to help women shed their
"feminine" curves and look more like men because men held
the political power. These diets were a social protest that
began in the early 1900s as women fought for the right to
vote. Yes, diets were used as a political statement!

Today people often diet without questioning why. They
just know that a certain weight is fashionable, and they want
to be fashionable so they'll be accepted. Some women are
always on a diet as a matter of course. To make the situation

worse, some societies now suffer from an epidemic of obesity. Many nutrition experts believe there is a strong correlation between obesity and dieting. So many diets and theories about dieting have confused us, wrecked our health, and wasted precious years as we've struggled to deal with food issues.

God wants you to be blessed by food and be at peace with food. He wants you to eat and be satisfied so you'll be strong and able to serve others. He wants you to be thankful and receive food as a blessing from Him. Oh how He must grieve when we badmouth food and our bodies that He created.

What will it take for you to begin to view food as a blessing and give thanks for it and your body? Perhaps you need to consider letting go of diets and any unreasonable demands you make regarding your appearance and appetite. Do you need to focus more on God's plan and less on man-made laws and standards?

Lord, I don't want my enemy—Satan, the father of lies—to trick me into starving myself for love and acceptance. Give me the desire to learn about healthy foods and purpose to eat better. I want to cultivate an attitude of gratitude for the blessings of this body You created and the food You provide.

Accepting Ourselves

As the heavens are higher than the earth,
so are my ways higher than your ways
and my thoughts than your thoughts.

Isaiah 55:9

A recent Dove campaign study "shows that women are less satisfied with their beauty than with almost every other dimension of life except their financial success."[4] A woman might be a success at the office, be beloved by her children and husband, be a valued member of the community, be a cherished friend, and be content in every aspect of her life but still be unhappy about her looks.

We have achieved such great heights in all aspects of life. Nothing is impossible for today's women except, it seems, self-acceptance. Do you wonder why this is? Why do we rack up accomplishments and accolades only to grimace at reflections in the mirror? Why do we refuse to let ourselves off the hook?

The degree to which we berate our appearance is related to the degree to which we are enslaved to an atheistic view of beauty. In a world without God, beauty is the source of good things and happy feelings. In a world with God, beauty is defined first as the condition of our spirits, and second as an expression of God's passionate creativity. As believers we allow God room to work without judgment. So we need to remember to not fret and frown when we look in the mirror because we know God designed us and we trust Him.

Lord, You've chosen to birth me into an era of unprecedented opportunities for women. I can achieve so much, focus on anything I choose, go anywhere, do whatever You set in my heart. And yet I know I criticize Your work by complaining that my body and appearance don't measure up to what I want. I'm sorry, Lord. Grant me more grace to look into a mirror and wink and smile at Your handiwork.

God Has a Plan for You

*Let a search be made for beautiful young
virgins for the king...and let beauty treatments
be given to them. Then let the girl who
pleases the king be queen instead of Vashti.*

ESTHER 2:2-4

After years of intense dieting, I was too thin and very miserable. I was every ounce as unhappy as I'd been before I started the dieting regime. *If I'm at my "perfect" weight, why is everything else still so imperfect?* I thought. In despair I realized all my dieting attempts were wasted. It wasn't my appearance that was making me unhappy and unfulfilled—it was my heart. I was knee-deep in insecurity, envy, and pride. No number on the scale could fix what was broken in my heart.

"Why?" I asked God. "Why did You create me like this? Why don't I look like a supermodel?" I felt God's answer in my spirit right then: "Because I didn't call you to be a supermodel."

Ouch.

I find hope in the story of Queen Esther. She was forced to compete with hundreds of beautiful young women to win the heart of a lusty king. Unbeknown to Esther but no secret to God was that the fate of the Jewish nation would rest on the king's choice. While we don't know what Esther looked like, we know she pleased the king's officials and the king more than any other woman. Something about her appealed to his tastes perfectly.

Do you think God had all this in mind when He created Esther? I do. Esther was created with specific beauty for a specific plan. She was created, as her Uncle Mordecai conjectured, "for such a time as this" (Esther 4:14).

You are like Esther in that you were created for "such a time as this." God gave you a body and appearance that fits His plans for your life. He intends to bless you, and if you will submit to His plan, He will bless and deliver others through your life.

Lord, there is so much at stake. When I look in the mirror or jump on a scale, remind me that You have a plan. Use me as You please to bless me and deliver into Your freedom the people around me who are in chains.

The Beauty of Contentment

*When the woman saw that the fruit of
the tree was good for food and pleasing
to the eye, and also desirable for gaining
wisdom, she took some and ate it.*

GENESIS 3:6

Like Esther, God created me for "just such a time as this": this life, these people, this era, and this place. He created me exactly how He wanted, and He will provide everything I need to accomplish His will. He gives me everything I need to have a peace-filled, love-filled heart. So why do I find myself wishing for more? Some days I wonder if I am less like Esther and more like Eve! I may have all the promises of paradise, but I can't resist reaching for just a little bit more. Although God wants me to avoid harming myself through crash diets, crazy surgeries, and desperate attempts to "improve" on His work, sometimes I read about those alternatives and they are pleasing to my eye. I imagine the benefits they offer and consider how much better my life might be if I tried them out.

What is in our human hearts that breeds this discontent? We know there is sin in the world, and we often harbor sin in our hearts. We know we have an enemy who delights in pulling us away from God. But I wonder if the hunger for perfection is really a longing for heaven, a cry in the depths of our spirits for God's perfection to return and rule the earth once more. Even as I acknowledge God's sovereign rule in designing my life and my appearance, I have to acknowledge that some part of me will always want more. I believe some part of will cry out for perfection, and that is a longing I will carry forever. I will not be free of it until I am perfected in body and spirit, made whole and complete in the presence of God.

Like Eve, we are surrounded by the promises of paradise. Even in the midst of pain and death, we live amid God's grace, mercy, love, and affection. May He help us to practice contentment so we don't destroy our peace by reaching for what was never meant for us. Let's ask the Holy Spirit to help us be content as we are even as we long for more.

> *Lord, help me practice the heavenly art of contentment as I wait for Your perfection to complete me. Show me how to celebrate Your presence right here, right now, and know that I am blessed just as I am. When I am tempted to reach for something I'm not meant to have, draw me back to Your plan.*

Stand Strong!

*God told the serpent: "Because you've
done this, you're cursed, cursed beyond all
cattle and wild animals, cursed to slink
on your belly and eat dirt all your life. I'm
declaring war between you and the Woman,
between your offspring and hers."*

GENESIS 3:14-15 MSG

This week you'll see more than 2000 images of alleged beauty ideals. More than 2000 times you will be told what beautiful is. Think of it this way: 2000 times this week someone will hand you a report card. And your grades are going to reflect how well you compare to the "standard" set by the culture. And worldly beauty does not grade on a curve: You either have it or you'd better get to the mall.

If you feel like you are under attack, it's because you are. When Eve confessed that she'd eaten the forbidden fruit after being enticed by the serpent, God cursed the serpent for all time. God declared war between the serpent and woman—the first war ever declared on earth. The serpent, whom we also know as the father of lies, is at war with you. His plans are to lure you into despair and defeat, to trick you and shame you.

But you, darling daughter of the King of kings, are safe. When the Spirit of Christ lives in your heart, you are reborn into eternal life. Satan's power and the deathly hold of sin in your life are broken forever. Your enemy's only weapon now is distraction. He can't destroy you, he can only try to shift your focus away from God's truth. One way he attempts to do this is by harassing you about your appearance. If he can keep you frustrated, he can keep you from being fruitful. If he can get you to accept a lie, you might bypass an important truth.

So this week, as you encounter the 2000 "innocent" suggestions that perhaps you don't measure up, remember: There is a war going on, and your heart is the coveted prize. Stand strong in Christ!

Lord, sometimes I accept the world's definition of beauty without even thinking about it. Beauty is often used as a weapon to shame and intimidate me. Help me never back down from Satan's lies by clinging to You and the truth that You love me.

The New You

*Whoever drinks the water I give him
will never thirst. Indeed, the water
I give him will become in him a spring
of water welling up to eternal life.*

JOHN 4:14

As you read this book, I'm praying that the truths of God's Word will seep deep into your heart and spirit so that springs of living water are bubbling up. I pray that debris is being cleared away so the living water can pour forth and minister to a hurting world.

What is your prayer? As you read this book, what are you hoping God will do in your life? Perhaps you want to be free of a bad habit, destructive thoughts, or critical comparisons. Freedom from those is a wonderful gift to ask for.

Sometimes we have hidden expectations we need to confess and get rid of. As you read about beauty and renew your mind, and as God heals your wounds (obvious and secret), what do you want your healing to look like? I catch myself hoping that as God heals me, I'll suddenly wake up in a tiny body and crave carrots instead of chocolate. I'll develop strong nails, clear skin, and a sleek rear end a quarter could bounce off of. Avoid this trap. Realize that the "healed and whole" version of yourself may still look a lot like you do now. Consider this wonderful quote from John Ortberg in his book *The Me I Want to Be*:

> As God helps you grow, you will change, but you will always be you. An acorn can grow into an oak tree, but it cannot become a rose bush. It can be a healthy oak or it can be a stunted oak—but it won't be a shrub. You will always be you—a growing, healthy you or a languishing you—but God did not create you to be anybody else.

Lord, please heal me and make my heart whole no matter what the end result will look like on the outside. Set me free to become who You created me to be.

Healing and Wholeness

My people have committed two sins:
They have forsaken me, the spring of living water,
and have dug their own cisterns,
broken cisterns that cannot hold water.

JEREMIAH 2:13

In biblical days, cisterns were small wells made of stone. They held a modest amount of water and often belonged to particular families. A good analogy is to think of a well as a large jug and a cistern as a cup. How do you know when a cup has a hole in it? When you pour the water in and notice a puddle forming around the outside of the bottom of the cup. A hole means your efforts and resources are being wasted every time the cup is used. It doesn't matter how fresh and pure the water is because your cup can't hold it. It doesn't matter how much you love that cup, what you paid for it, or how long you've carried it around. It's broken and useless.

In today's verse, God warns us against using broken cisterns to hold His living water. The people have sinned against God by forsaking Him, the source of all living water. They dug cisterns that couldn't hold water, much less God's *living* water. The tragedy here isn't just that the people walked away from God, but that they also wasted so much energy, time, and resources.

We're no different. We dig broken cisterns every day, and then we blame God for making us thirsty. How can we avoid making the mistake God's people did according to today's verse? We have to find the broken cisterns in our lives and replace them with God's cisterns that hold His living water!

Lord, forgive me when I've forsaken You. Sometimes I do things my own way, wasting my time and resources and straying from the plans You have for me. Today I give You my broken cups and cisterns. Please replace them with Your cistern filled with Your living water.

Giving Thanks

I praise you because I am fearfully and
wonderfully made; your works are
wonderful, I know that full well.

PSALM 139:14

ears spilled down my cheeks as I watched the action hero outrun the bad guys just as a jumbo jet crashed to the ground and the terrorists jumped out to safety. My husband leaned over and whispered, "I know. I always cry at this part too." I groaned at his bad joke. I wasn't crying because of the macho action we were watching. I was weeping because the action hero was running—something I wasn't able to do. I had undergone serious surgery on my ankle and was still unable to walk without assistance. I had gone from finishing my first triathlon and half-marathon to using a walker to get to the bathroom. The doctor said it would be a year before I could *try* to run again—and even then I might not be able to. So here I was watching someone run and being mesmerized by the beauty of it. Had I ever fully appreciated the gift of movement before? Had I praised God for giving me legs that worked? I hope I did.

We've been given so much. Our imperfect bodies are

capable of such beauty. We really are miracles. Having lost the ability to walk and run for a time, I am deeply appreciative of the creative way God made us. I want to overwhelm my critical inner voices with praises for God for what I can do. I am a miracle, and you are too.

Lord, I praise You because I am wonderfully and fearfully made. David was a mighty man with plenty of power, money, and love, yet he still took the time to praise You for his capable body. I also thank You for everything I can do and for this body.

Beauty in Laughter

*He will yet fill your mouth with laughter and
your lips with shouts of joy.*

JOB 8:21

went in recently for my first mammogram. The doctors spied some suspicious spots and recommended several biopsies. As they performed each biopsy, they left a tiny titanium metal marker at each site. This way they could track any changes over time for accurate diagnosis and follow-up care. Thankfully the biopsies were negative for cancer, and life went back to normal. That is, until another doctor recommended I have a routine health screening done at a local hospital. I wasn't thrilled, to say the least. I hate hospitals. I despise the loss of privacy and all the little indignities. Prior to the exam, a nurse went over my chart, asking me about any preexisting medical conditions or surgeries.

"Are you a smoker?" she asked.

"No," I replied.

"Any history of diabetes or high cholesterol?"

"No."

"Any implants or metal in your body?"

"I have titanium implants in both breasts," I confessed.

Her jaw dropped and her gaze lowered. She was trying to maintain a professional demeanor, but she had never heard of titanium implants, and I could see the wheels turning in her mind as she imagined what metal breast implants were like. By the time I finished explaining what the micro implants were for, we were both nearly hysterical with laughter. I'm sure she thought someone had invented a new cure for sagging breasts. I was blushing beet red when I left the hospital that day, but all that laughter had brightened my perspective about the hospital considerably. Isn't laughter wonderful? It means we're alive and fully aware that God's strength will make life okay. It means we can laugh at our weaknesses because we know we're loved.

Lord, I need to laugh more often. I take myself so seriously some days. Sometimes, Lord, teach me through laughter. Heal me through giggles and smiles and whispered jokes. Show me the joy that's waiting for me today.

Accepting Love

Surely goodness and love will follow me
all the days of my life, and I will dwell
in the house of the LORD forever.

PSALM 23:6

was looking through the sales catalog of my favorite clothing brand, daydreaming about how beautiful I would look and feel if only I had hundreds of dollars to spend on new clothes. My husband snuck up behind me and planted a kiss on top of my head. Without looking at him, I reached my hand up to shoo him away. Immediately the irony of the moment pierced my heart. I was daydreaming about feeling beautiful and how, if I felt and looked that beautiful, life would be better. And surely I'd be more loveable. I was so focused on that, that when authentic love snuck up to me I almost missed it. I didn't need new clothes to be beautiful in my man's eyes. I was already beautiful to him. But I almost rejected him and his real love in favor of a fantasy. I almost rejected the love that was offered freely because I was daydreaming about how I could earn it.

Why did I center on earning love instead of freely accepting the love that was offered? Do you struggle with this too? I suspect most of us do. I remember when a church near my home tried to do a "free" garage sale. They marked all the items as "free." I didn't see anyone shopping when I drove by, and I didn't want to stop either. We're suspicious of things given away. We wonder what's wrong with the items or worry that people will think we need charity. We feel better about ourselves if we earn what we want. "Pay your own way," is our mantra.

God won't let us earn His love. He's not going to let us work for it just so we'll feel better about ourselves. This love isn't about us; it's about Him. When God wants to give us something freely, we need to accept the gift just as we are, just where we stand. We should be awed and humbled at His great gifts. Real love is like that too because it comes from God.

Lord, am I trying to earn what You want to give me? I know I can't earn Your love, so help me give up trying. I can be confident and happy because You love me, Lord. With Your grace, I will gladly accept the gifts You give today.

The End Is Written

He will wipe every tear from their eyes.
There will be no more death or
mourning or crying or pain.

REVELATION 21:4

How do you read a novel? Some people are methodical. They start on page one and read all the way through to the back cover, reading in sequential order. Some people can't wait for the ending, so they start there. If they like the ending, they go to page one and start reading. For some, the ending is not as important as experiencing the whole story. For others, the ending is the only reason to read, and if the ending isn't good, why bother with the rest of it?

We live like that too. Some of us are content to let the story of our lives unfold at their own pace, and some of us want to know the ending up front. We want to be assured that we'll retire with a pot of gold, our children will be successful and outlive us, and that we'll jump into eternity where loves ones are waiting.

Let me offer a word of reassurance: We can't know our full story, but we do know the Author and Master story creator and storyteller. We know God loves us and has many blessings in store for us. We know we're safe even when the storms rage. We know we'll "win," even when the enemy seems to be momentarily getting the best of us. We don't understand everything, but we can be confident that our Creator isn't just aimlessly writing and mumbling: He's building to a beautiful conclusion, a breathtaking ending.

I don't know your specific struggle today, but I can promise you that a wonderful ending is yours. You're going to be okay. God will work everything out in a way that trades any brokenness for tremendous blessing through Jesus Christ.

Lord, sometimes what drives me to make mistakes is my fear for the future. I want to know now my story will have a happy ending. You are the Creator Author. Remind me to trust You, and help me rely on Your wisdom, grace, and mercy today.

God's Beautiful Design

You created my inmost being;
you knit me together in my mother's womb.

PSALM 139:13

Did you know that women's hips are set at a different angle than men's? This unique design is what gives us our distinctly feminine walk. God designed our bodies to be quite unique, and He delights in us.

Femininity is often associated with weakness, but it wasn't always this way. Prior to the Industrial Revolution, women who were strong and stout made good wives. They could handle the enormous burdens of birthing babies, helping to run a farm, making clothes, grinding grains, and slaughtering livestock. Superhuman strength was desirable. A man prized his strong, capable wife. After the Industrial Revolution, when clothes, soaps, and food were made available for purchase, women's roles in the home shifted. Suddenly "weak" women came into vogue. Fainting couches became popular. A woman who did nothing all day but wear expensive gowns and lie around became a status symbol. Because most women weren't career oriented and the work in the home had been reduced, many had no dynamic vision for themselves or their daughters. They didn't recognize their potential.

Today we have almost the opposite problem. We suffer from an abundance of opportunity and much confusion over roles. We want to be feminine but we're not always sure what that means in every situation. We want to be beautiful, but we're not sure which cultural expectations we should let go of.

Lord, many of my expectations about my femininity have been handed down from women who faced different struggles than I do. Help me honor their lives by trusting You to call forth the best and brightest version of me I can be. I entrust my womanhood to You knowing You delight in the way You designed me.

Beauty and Spirituality

Your beauty should not come from outward adornment, such as braided hair and the wearing of gold jewelry and fine clothes.

1 Peter 3:3

In the ancient world, beauty and spirituality were intertwined. Ancient Egyptians believed that beauty made a person more godlike. For ancient Jewish women, bathing and applying aromatic oils were routine for preparing for worship. And in many cults, women would paint idols with cosmetics and then paint their own faces to match. Some scholars speculate this was what the infamous Jezebel was doing when she painted her eyes just before Jehu came calling (2 Kings 9:30). Jezebel was paying homage to her god.

Beauty and spirit have always been joined in our hearts and imaginations. I believe we instinctively understand that our outward appearance reflects our inner condition. Whether we're hungry for attention or want to disappear into a crowd, our appearance usually communicates this message. And this seems to be a universal, timeless practice. We may feel a little hesitant to admit that there is a strong spiritual component to beauty because we don't want to repeat the Egyptian's mistake of believing physical beauty can bring eternal rewards. However, when we acknowledge the spiritual aspect, an important door is opened in our hearts. We invite God to move into this area and cleanse and heal old wounds. We take a natural instinct—the desire for beauty—and offer it to the Lord as an invitation for Him to reveal His love in us and through us.

The source of our beauty should not come, as the Bible says, from our outward adornment. Rather, the source of our radiance is the great love poured out on us by Christ. When our hearts overflow with His love and peace, we also experience beauty as a spiritual reality, as an overflow of joy that lets our spirits dance in Christ's freedom at the foot of the cross.

Lord, so many place their faith in their appearance and suffer from wretched self-images. Beauty comes from You, and all beauty leads to You. My heart finds rest and fulfillment in and through You.

Real Beauty

*God saw all that he had made,
and it was very good.*

GENESIS 1:31

*I*f you read a dictionary's definition of beauty, you'll find a word used often is "harmony." Beauty is the pleasing sum of different parts working together. In the old languages, especially Latin, harmony meant "agreement." So the root definition of physical beauty, then, is not a scale or set of measurements and colors. Rather, physical beauty is revealed through a woman in agreement and who radiates harmony.

Do you know women like that? I sure do. I rarely notice whether their clothes are in style or their nails are perfect. Instead I sense the inner calm they exude, the sense they are comfortable in their own skin and take good care of themselves. They don't try to whip themselves into a certain size or stay a certain age; they just live…and live gracefully. These harmonious women send a silent, secret message to every woman in their lives: It's okay to be who you are, just as you are. Accept yourself and allow all your being to exist in harmony. Shame and self-criticism are banished. They have no home in the heart of a woman in agreement with her God and Creator.

When we embrace ourselves as we are and are willing to live in harmony with our design, we agree with God that His works are indeed good.

> *Lord, I want to be a woman in agreement with You. Help me experience harmony and peace. I want to walk in a freedom that is life-changing. Use me to offer this healing to other women so they will discover the way to You.*

Beauty in Wisdom

*The wise woman builds her house,
but with her own hands the
foolish one tears hers down.*

PROVERBS 14:1

What's the craziest thing you've ever done for beauty? When I was an actress, I got a call to audition for a rock music video. I wanted to look as skinny as possible, and I didn't own a girdle, so I used electrical tape to strap down my hips. I was board-straight and thought it was a good look.

When I arrived at the location, the director's assistant told me the audition included wearing a bikini because the video was going to be shot next to a pool. I swallowed in fear. I knew I had about two rolls of electrical tape strapped on underneath my skirt. That day I experienced my first and most painful bikini line hair removal. Laugh if you want to, but I know I am not the first woman to harm herself in her pursuit of perfection. Consider these words from my dear friend novelist Siri Mitchell:

> In Elizabethan England, when Queen Elizabeth I de-
> cided that she didn't like her pockmarks and was tired

of her wrinkles, she started slathering lead-based cosmetics onto her face. [This] caused her skin to age more quickly and her hair and teeth to fall out, and may have eventually caused the blood poisoning which killed her. But the women in her court happily followed her lead, bleaching their hair red in imitation of hers and applying lead paint to their own skin. An entire generation of women was harmed by one queen's overweening vanity.

Throughout the ages, women have risked humiliation and worse in pursuit of beauty. We've cut off toes, maimed our feet by binding them, displaced internal organs with tight corsets, taken poison, and swallowed tapeworms. We've done some pretty ugly things to be beautiful. If you're ever tempted to believe that beauty is a trivial matter, remember that countless women have sacrificed their health and dignity for beauty. God wants to reach those women with a message of hope, and He wants to reach you too.

Lord, beauty matters to me as a woman. Meet me here in this desire and longing. Protect me from the foolishness of my culture and the mistakes so many women have made. I want my beauty to be an expression of Your love for me and through me.

A WOMAN'S PATH TO INNER BEAUTY

Beauty in Discipline

He who heeds discipline shows the way to life,
but whoever ignores correction leads others astray.

PROVERBS 10:17

Beauty seems very self-centered, doesn't it? It's a me-me-me industry. But really, beauty impacts more than just us. I find it fascinating that the Bible warns us that our actions impact a wide circle of bystanders.

Beauty requires discipline, and when I contemplate self-discipline, I always consider how it will impact *my* life. In today's verse, we see that God is concerned with how my self-discipline will impact others. We lead others, often without meaning to, by many of the decisions we make.

Younger women and girls are watching us for cues on how to be a woman, how we define beauty, and what we consider its level of importance. If we can't find the will to reject false standards and embrace ourselves as beautiful just how God created us, we are not merely hurting ourselves. We're also inadvertently taking hostages and leading people astray. However, when we live in freedom in Christ and allow Him to express His unique, passionate design in and through us, we show the next generation how to honor our heavenly

Father. We show the next generation how to define beauty and experience abundance, courage, and grace.

It's never too late to accept ourselves with humility, humor, and trust. This acceptance is a form a spiritual self-discipline. Yes, it doesn't come easily to most of us—discipline rarely does. But its rewards are great. And when we embrace discipline for the sake of others, the rewards are eternal.

Lord, beauty and discipline are not just about me. In this world obsessed with physical perfection there are so many hurting women and girls. Help me show them how to find You. I praise You for making me so perfectly imperfect so people will know You are my source of peace, joy, and beauty.

God's Economy

"For I know the plans I have for you," declares
the LORD, "plans to prosper you and not to
harm you, plans to give you hope and a future."

JEREMIAH 29:11

*I*n God's economy, nothing is wasted. I hope you
haven't experienced the pain of rejection, but if you
have, please let me encourage you. God is leading you into
a wonderful and wonderfully important future. He will not
waste those moments when you felt the pain of not fitting
in, the agony of feeling self-conscious, and the heartbreak of
being lonely. God knew those days would come into your
life. He is a God who makes plans, and He has a plan to
prosper you, to give you a hope and a future that is better
than anything your imagination is capable of creating. God
wants something better and bolder for you than you can
know right now.

If you've felt the pain of being different, God may be
giving you a special compassion for outsiders. If you've suffered the pain of not measuring up, let God use this as the
reminder to stay away from the tyranny of perfection. Whatever you've suffered, whatever labels you've endured and

battles you've faced, God has a plan. None of your suffering will be wasted. He will return goodness for your pain and provide healing for your wounds.

> *Lord, is there any other religion or god who can offer me such redemption, such assurance, such grace? No! Your plans for me are far more detailed, more powerful, and more blessed than I know. Unlock a river of blessings into my life. Transform my past pain into means to reach out to others in Your name.*

Our Best Feature

He who guards his lips guards his life,
but he who speaks rashly will come to ruin.

PROVERBS 13:3

Above all else, guard your heart,
for it is the wellspring of life.

PROVERBS 4:23

eauty magazines admonish women to choose their best feature and play it up. We're taught how to dress and accessorize so that others notice our "best" feature. This feature might be our eyes, our legs, our lips, our figures. We often consider it the best because it holds the most potential to attain favor according to the world's definition of beauty.

Did you know that God has His eyes on two of our features in particular? He is deeply concerned with our lips and our hearts. Their potential to give or destroy life is immense. Notice today's verses from Proverbs. If we guard our lips, we guard our lives. If we guard our hearts, we guard the "wellspring" that our lives flow from.

Wellsprings are the source of water that feeds a well. And wells are useless if their source dries up or becomes polluted.

So too our hearts feed our lives. If they become polluted or dried out, we have nothing to offer. Protecting our hearts means we are very careful about what or who we allow ourselves to become close to. It's always harder to disentangle our hearts rather than stop them from becoming attached in the first place. But guarding both our lips and our hearts requires discipline in a world gone wild. We can expect to feel some pain and discomfort when we put discipline into practice, but afterward we will experience the priceless peace of a life well lived.

The world might consider certain physical features as our most-valued assets, but God makes His perfect wisdom clear: Our lips and our hearts have the greatest powers to bless or destroy. How we speak and what and who we love determine the quality of our lives much more than physical characteristics.

Lord, help me watch what I say so I don't harbor sin or grumble. Let me be a conduit for Your life-giving water. Give me Your refreshing comfort and wisdom to share with others.

Honoring God and Others

Flee from sexual immorality. All other sins
a man commits are outside his body, but he
who sins sexually sins against his own body.

1 CORINTHIANS 6:18

"I'm not hurting anybody," she argued. "This is just who I am, how I express myself." Whether these are the words of a 13-year-old girl or a 30-year-old woman makes no difference. Woman of all ages dress provocatively, exposing a great deal of cleavage, thigh, and midriff. They present a highly sexualized version of themselves to a world of strangers. Is it true that the way we dress hurts no one? Is it all innocent self-expression? According to the nonprofit group Polaris Project, "The average age of entry into prostitution is 12-13 years old in the U.S. An estimated 200,000 American children are at high risk for trafficking into the sex industry each year."[5]

In many countries sexuality has been divorced from intimacy. When we dress provocatively in public, we promote anonymous sexuality as a commodity. We support the idea that sex is not naturally attached to intimacy, and that sexuality outside of marriage is a valid method of self-expression.

We allow the purchasers and abusers of pornography to justify their desires and their acts.

We are our sisters' keepers, and we have great responsibility to protect all women and children (and even boys and men) from exploitation. When we're alone in our dressing rooms and closets, we choose how we dress, but the impact of our decisions are felt by many. May we be the women who challenge a fallen world's idea of sexuality and desirability by bringing in God's values to show the path to true love and intimacy.

Lord, physical sexuality is so pervasive in the world that seduction has become a public pastime. Help me live a bold, righteous life that honors You and compassionately reveals Your truths. Give me insights for sharing the beauty and intimacy of sexuality as You created it to be.

From Sorrow Comes Celebration

*Suppose a woman has ten silver coins and
loses one. Does she not light a lamp, sweep the
house and search carefully until she finds it?*

LUKE 15:8

A riddle: When you are looking for a lost item, why do you always find it in the last place you look? Do you know the answer?

When you're looking for something, it doesn't really matter how hard you look or how long you look. What really matters is *where* you look. If you're not looking in the right spot, you won't find what you're looking for. Ever. In the parable of the lost coin, as told by Jesus and recorded in Luke 15, the woman looked in the right place and found the coin. (Yes, that's the answer to the riddle. If you found the coin, you quit looking, making it the "last place you looked.") The parable would have had quite a different message if the woman had searched in the market or in the fields. Because she was looking in the right place, she was successful in recovering the coin and could rejoice. The angst of her loss was replaced by exquisite joy.

Isn't this comforting? Your search for fulfillment, your

longing to be beautiful and the sorrows and shames of not measuring up, can be replaced with inexpressible joy. You can find what you're searching for. In fact, you're looking in the right spot at this very moment as you take a moment to sit with the Lord and consider thoughts and wisdom based on His Word. You have known suffering, but you will also know great joy!

Lord, only You can take my sorrows and shames and turn them into causes for celebration. You are a God of miracles and amazing mercies. Thank You for Your generous outpouring of grace into my life.

God's Divine Power

*His divine power has given us everything
we need for life and godliness through our
knowledge of him who called us by his own
glory and goodness. Through these he has given
us his very great and precious promises, so
that through them you may participate in
the divine nature and escape the corruption
in the world caused by evil desires.*

2 PETER 1:3-4

Have you ever wondered what drives a beauty trend? As pornography becomes a worldwide obsession, the startling truth is that porn decides what's pretty. Surgically enhanced porn stars are setting the standards for women. Science even confirmed this. In 2007, the *British Medical Journal* reported that women were seeking cosmetic surgery on their genitals, and the authors suggested that the surgeries were requested in order to match images from pornography. Another survey found that teens who viewed online porn also researched breast augmentation and collagen implants.[6]

Even if pornography is never allowed in your home, it still impacts your life. Every time you turn on the television or flip through a magazine you're viewing images of women who have been remodeled surgically based on what is popular in porn.

Society seems to be in a free-fall decline, and much of the corruption focuses around women. God's definitions of beauty and sexuality are under constant attack. Thankfully we have such great hope and encouragement in Christ. God has issued an invitation to us to "participate in the divine nature"! We can escape corruption. We can be healed and whole.

When we make a choice to embrace our beauty as reflections of God's tastes instead of pornography's, we participate in the divine nature. When we speak words of encouragement that reflect God's views of femininity and sexuality to young girls, we participate in the divine nature. What an incredible gift we've been given.

Lord, this world needs Your divine touch. I am awed that You invite me to participate in Your work—loving people and leading them to redemption and peace in You. I pray that Your healing will rest upon me today. Give me words of encouragement I can share.

God Says You're Beautiful

The king is enthralled by your beauty;
honor him, for he is your lord.

Psalm 45:11

God doesn't think you're just pretty. He doesn't think you are just attractive. No, my sister, He is *enthralled* by your beauty. He's absolutely charmed by you. The God who sees our deepest secrets and hidden thoughts, bad habits, and blunders, is telling us in today's verse that He finds us captivating.

I know for some of us this truth is hard to receive. Our first impulse is to discount it, to add a "Yeah, but…" at the end. We flat-out don't believe it. We may be able to agree that it's a lovely sentiment, but we can't quite accept that it's meant for us or is about us.

I encourage you to put this verse on an index card and read the words before you go to sleep every night this week. Close your eyes and let the words work their way through your thoughts, your concerns, and your tensions. Receive the words as a love letter from your Lord.

We honor God by believing Him. And it's important that we don't just believe a portion of what He says about us.

We've got to drop the "Yes, but…" from our mind-set. I know this from experience. A woman I know recently stopped by to ask about something I'd witnessed. I told her the truth, and she screamed, "You're lying!" I wasn't. She seemed willing to accept other statements I'd made, but not everything I said. We had no harmony at all. The relationship is clouded now because she refuses to believe part of my answer.

> *Lord, I understand that disbelief can cloud a relationship. Yet when I look in the mirror, I feel silly believing You are enthralled with me. I want to embrace all Your truths. Please help my disbelief and show me how to honor You as my Lord.*

Victory in Beauty

*When an evil spirit comes out of a man, it
goes through arid places seeking rest and
does not find it. Then it says, "I will return
to the house I left." When it arrives, it finds
the house unoccupied, swept clean and put
in order. Then it goes and takes with it seven
other spirits more wicked than itself, and
they go in and live there. And the final
condition of that man is worse than the first.*

MATTHEW 12:43-45

The message we hear daily as women is deceptively simple. If we don't feel beautiful, we're not trying hard enough. If we don't look beautiful, we're not spending enough. We can be tempted to run the opposite direction just to escape. Some people give up on appearance completely to avoid the pressure to attain unrealistic results. We declare ourselves to be independent of any worldly standard or ideas about beauty. We refuse to play the game. I love what Beth Moore, in her book *Breaking Free,* has to say about finding victory:

> God wants us to be victors. We don't become victors
> by conquering the enemy. We become victors through

surrender to Christ. We don't become victors by our independence from the enemy. We become victors by our dependence on God.

We can't find relief from the pressures of the world by retiring and hiding. We can't escape unrealistic beauty ideals by giving up on our appearance entirely. The only way we can escape the tyranny of worldly beauty expectations and move into freedom is through surrender and dependence on God, who has different standards and ideals.

As human beings, we are created to want God's moral order. We're created to need standards and ideals. So if we're going to reject the world's set of standards, we need to have a new set to put in its place. It's said that nature abhors a vacuum, and the basis for this is, I believe, found in today's scripture. If we want to root out unrealistic expectations and ideals, that's wonderful. But while you're cleaning house, consider carefully what you will put in to replace what you take out. Your choices may be the source of much peace or much unrest for years to come.

Lord, walk closely with me on this journey. When the time comes to clean out an old stronghold, show me immediately what to replace it with. Shower me with better, brighter visions and goals. I choose to walk more closely with You every day.

Trusting God

*When the angel of the LORD appeared to Gideon,
he said, "The LORD is with you, mighty warrior."
"But sir," Gideon replied, "if the LORD is with us,
why has all this happened to us?"*

JUDGES 6:12-13

We are always welcome to petition God about our interests and concerns, including beauty and body issues. But what if He answered your prayers, not with what was "best" for you, but what was best for others? Would you be willing to accept His answer?

Maybe God has a different ideal for your weight, or your nose, or your shape than you do—and not because He doesn't love you, but because He loves other people as well. Perhaps He wants you to live free and whole just as you are, lighting the way for others who are scared and hurting as they struggle with the same issues you have. If you've prayed and asked God to change something and it hasn't happened yet, one possible reason is that He wants to answer your prayer on a much larger scale. The peace you seek for yourself might be made available to the people around you instead.

Have you ever wondered whose side God is on? We see

other women with the features, beauty, abilities, or lifestyles we covet and wonder why they were blessed and not us. We question whether God is with us or not, whether He's looking out for us. "Why is life this way?" we ask Him.

God may not answer that question during your physical life on earth, but He does give us little hints, a little salve to soothe the wounds. There are bigger forces at play than you know. More is at stake than you can guess. You are a beloved, cherished, charming daughter of the King of kings. He created you with purpose. You are here to walk in the freedom of Christ and lead others into His freedom. God may be using the very things you aren't happy with to accomplish this. Take courage!

> *Lord, just as the Bible says, Your ways are not always my ways. Your design for me may not be what I would have chosen, but I know You love me. You created me for Your unique, blessed purposes, and I'm thankful to be part of Your plan.*

Peace with God's Plan

Woe to him who quarrels with his Maker...
Does the clay say to the potter,
"What are you making?"
Does your work say,
"He has no hands"?

ISAIAH 45:9

In the ancient world, pots were handmade and valued. They also conveyed important information about the potter. One artisan might use a unique paint design, while another might choose distinctive shapes. The pots revealed who the maker was.

I can't imagine a more humiliating experience for an artisan than to have a pot start talking back and insulting his or her skill. As God's creations, we're all guilty of exactly that. Criticism is almost a feminine sport. Think of it like tennis. We complain about our weight, which is like serving a tennis ball. The person we're talking to smacks it back to us, reassuring us with a nice comment about us but then adding her own remark about something she's dissatisfied with on her body. No one ever wins this game, but we all play it at times.

You and I are the raw material God has chosen to craft

into useful designs. We each bear the stamp of our Creator. We each reveal aspects of His identity. And we are each commanded to stop insulting Him by accusing Him of sloppy designs and bad proportions. God made birds fly and dolphins dance across the waves. Surely we do not dare to tell Him that He lacks skill. He is an artisan with no equal, and we are so blessed to be called His!

Lord, You put up with so much from me sometimes. You've given me a unique design that suits Your purposes. When I insult Your handiwork, gently remind me to stop. You are a wonderful artist, and I am so honored to be crafted by Your touch and created by Your love.

Promises to Keep

*Hezekiah turned his face to the wall and
prayed to the LORD, "Remember, O LORD,
how I have walked before you faithfully
and with wholehearted devotion and
have done what is good in your eyes."*

2 KINGS 20:2-3

ezekiah was a king in ancient Israel. He was near
death and begged for God's healing. God answered
his prayer by adding 15 years to his life. Hezekiah pledged to
live as a changed man, a vow he later didn't keep.

I understand Hezekiah. After I slip and God picks me
back up, I pledge to be a new woman. No more overeating,
laziness, sarcasm, or fake sincerity. I'll do everything different, even the things that aren't spiritually related, per se. No
more junk food or red meat—I'll only eat organic vegetables and soy burgers. I'll remember my sunscreen every day
and stop sleeping with my makeup on. This time, I pledge,
things will be different.

I'm exhausted before I'm even done praying, and I secretly
slip back into despair. I know I can't keep those promises no
matter how passionately I want to. Just as there's no sense

putting fuel in the wrong tank, there's no sense in pledging what we can't accomplish. Self-reliant pledges are misplaced energy.

It's not wrong to want to change or to try to change. But it is wrong to think we can do it by ourselves. When we do that we're rejecting God's energizing love in favor of rigorous programs of self-improvement.

"Thank You," I say to God in my heart, "for getting me this far. I'll take it from here! You'll be so impressed. I won't need Your help in this area again." It's so easy to forget that God wants to help us. He doesn't want us to walk down any path alone. Our Father in heaven wants us to be set free, but via His Spirit and through His working. He wants us to make the decision to trust in Him alone and release any fantasy about fixing ourselves through personal willpower. Willpower doesn't lead to lasting change, and neither do promises we can't keep. The power of God's Spirit, however, changes us in ways we can never imagine and opens opportunities to love and be loved.

> *Lord, I am tempted to try to make myself a new person. But the truth is that only through Your Spirit can real change happen. Transform me today through the power of Your love.*

Rejection and Redemption

*The stone the builders rejected has
become the capstone.*

PSALM 118:22

Rejection is painful to endure, isn't it? I experienced plenty growing up, and it breaks my heart when I see my children struggle through it. But I believe rejection can include great spiritual power. Consider the great heroes in the Bible. Most experienced long seasons of rejection before God's purposes and plans were revealed. Rejection meant refinement, and a refined person is someone God can use mightily.

When experiencing rejection, our first instinct is usually fight or flight. We lash out or coil into ourselves seeking protection. We need time to process the experience and patience as God untangles the mess it creates in our hearts. But if we're willing to trust in His overwhelming love, we know He will turn rejection into refinement. And the woman God chooses to refine, He also chooses to bless. You become a blessed woman who has much to offer others.

Is that what you want? Are you willing to endure the pain of rejection in exchange for greater ministry to others?

If you're still hesitant, here's one more bit of information: God often allows the most rejection, over the longest period of time, to those He has called to do great things. Esther suffered harem life for a full year before she was presented to the king. And, knowing how some women are, surely Esther experienced rejection from the other women, negative gossip, and loneliness. Moses was rejected by his own people and had to flee to a desert for years before he was called back by God (Acts 7:35). Jesus was scorned by the Jewish leaders and experts in Mosaic law. They even shouted Him down when He tried to speak and incited and hired people to discredit Him. Each of these people played an important role in delivering their people. (Jesus, of course, being the final and greatest.) These three people knew the pain of constant, ongoing rejection. And God used their experiences for His glory, just as He will use yours.

Lord, rejection is so painful, and I don't want to endure it. But I know I will because this is a fallen world filled with broken hearts. When I face rejection, remind me of Your truths. May any difficulties I experience pale in comparison to the riches of grace You have stored up for me and those around me.

Finding Balance

Don't you see that whatever enters the mouth
goes into the stomach and then out of the body?
But the things that come out of the mouth come
from the heart, and these make a man "unclean."
For out of the heart come evil thoughts, murder,
adultery, sexual immorality, theft, false testimony,
slander. These are what make a man "unclean."

MATTHEW 15:17-20

We lack balance in our culture. We feel uneasy discussing our bodies in spiritual terms, and yet we often slip unnoticed into the culture of body worship. Religious terms have even been hijacked by this new form of the old sin of self-worship. Food is no longer just food. Now we label it as "clean" or "unclean." In biblical days, this meant the food had been sacrificed to idols or forbidden by God. Today it means any food that detracts from a perfect physique, especially foods high in sugar or calories. Even among Christians, many have begun to believe that a thin person is holier (less sinful) than an overweight person.

Jesus knew our hearts were prone to confusion and deception. We are spiritual beings, and spiritual beings crave worship. In a culture disconnected from God, this craving becomes corrupt. We search for a philosophy, a celebrity, or an ideal to worship and pursue what makes us feel better and doesn't require sacrifice.

An additional danger for women in body worship is that the standard of perfection is so unnaturally thin. God designed your body to be efficient at storing fat. Fat protects your organs, helps balance your hormonal cycles, keeps your hair and skin lovely, and some types of fat even offer additional protection against heart disease. Women are built to carry more fat than men, and we often find it harder to lose fat when dieting. That's not a design flaw! It was God's intention.

We decide every day who or what we will worship. We can worship God and choose to be wise stewards of our bodies. We can disconnect from a toxic, confused culture and practice honoring God and His standards by honoring our bodies as His chosen temples.

Lord, my body is for You and for Your good plans and purposes. Help me have a discerning heart and use the best information from You so that I will be a wise steward of my body. May my spirit grow in You as I find rest in knowing You designed me with great care.

God's Temple

The priests then brought the ark of the LORD's
covenant to its place in the inner sanctuary
of the temple, the Most Holy Place, and
put it beneath the wings of the cherubim.

1 KINGS 8:6

What was the purpose of the Jewish temple in Old Testament times? It was a place where people could meet with the Lord. A place set apart and holy. A place for God's Spirit to dwell. A place where He could be petitioned. A place where He would answer the priests and give counsel, wisdom, and direction.

Inside this temple there was a special sanctuary called the "Most Holy Place" or "Holy of Holies." Only the high priest was allowed to enter it to meet with God. It was a place for intimate, one-on-one meetings.

In the New Testament God says we are His new temple. Our bodies were constructed as holy meeting places between our spirits and God's Spirit. The purpose of our bodies is not to gain worship for ourselves but to worship God in. I believe that inside each of our bodies is a Holy of Holies—a spiritual room, a private part of our spirits where we meet alone with

God. Our husbands, children, and friends can't enter. This is where God meets with each of us, one-on-one. This is where change happens in our spirits. How comforting to know that God has prearranged for quiet, intimate conversations with us! He has made provision to nourish and nurture us in the deepest part of our spirits, minds, and hearts.

This special sanctuary is ready and waiting for you at any time, day or night. When you're feeling bruised from the demands of this world, a world that sets your value by what it sees on the outside, you can retreat to this most Holy of Holies through reading Scripture and prayer.

Whatever we look like on the outside, each of us carries a sacred placed within, a meeting place for God. We can rest in the comfort that God cares for us and wants us to commune with Him.

> *Lord, the world values my body for its external appearance, but the best part of me is within. Thank You for being my God. You understand my need for comfort and encouragement. Thank You that our meeting place is shielded from the rest of the world. I love being alone with You.*

The Power of Community

Though one may be overpowered,
two can defend themselves. A cord of
three strands is not quickly broken.

ECCLESIASTES 4:12

I love what I once heard at a Steve Arterburn "Lose It for Life" conference: "If you could have done it by yourself, you would have." When a problem is born in isolation, it must be uprooted by fellowship. When you're secretly bingeing, purging, or living in silent shame of any kind, God would love to see you reach out to someone else for support. Share your secret. Ask someone to walk alongside you. Join a support group or find a counselor. The power of community is so much greater than our willpower and determination.

My life bears witness to this. I wanted to be a "real runner," but I didn't make much progress until I invited two athletic women to meet me every Saturday morning for a run. When we started, I was so slow when I jogged that they walked beside me. Today, we have participated in races of all lengths and types. I even beat one of my friends! (Okay, she was injured during the race, but I knew a good chance when I saw one.) These women have been the ones I've spilled my "private" sins to, the sins I struggled with alone for so long. When an old boyfriend began contacting me, these women listened to my thoughts and temptations. When the economy went sour, I explained my financial situation, and they made suggestions about what services I could eliminate. If it were not for these women and the community we formed, I would have ended up broke, out-of-shape, and handling a troubled marriage alone.

Because I invited a community into my isolation, I walked through those circumstances in peace and freedom. Sin lost its terror, and temptation lost its allure. Please don't underestimate the power of community. When we reach out to others, we open our arms to healing.

Lord, isolation can feel good even while it's destroying my life and feeding the power of sin. You have surrounded me with godly women who will walk with me if only I dare ask. Help me have the courage to reach out.

Exit Strategies

*Make us glad for as many days as
you have afflicted us for as many
years as we have seen trouble.*

PSALM 90:15

inancial experts ask clients to devise an "exit strategy" *before* investing in the market to ensure that a client makes the highest profit and/or suffers minimal loss. Whatever your struggle, whether an eating disorder, a poor self-image, or jealousy, take a few moments today to create your own exit strategy. For instance,

- When this trial is over, what do you want to have gained? Wisdom? Influence? Compassion?

- What losses will you work to minimize? Health? Relationships? Career?

- Because you walked this road, how do you want your future to be blessed?

- What will you have to offer future generations of women?

I believe God is the ultimate economist. In His economy, nothing is wasted, forgotten, or overlooked. He has counted every hair on your head, every tear you have cried, and numbered every day you will live. Nothing about you and your life escapes His attention. He has all knowledge of you, and because He loves you He plans to bless you richly. He will redeem your days of suffering if you'll let Him. He can turn your sorrows into victories, your struggles into incredible strengths.

I believe you can ask God what your exit strategy should be. What are the blessings and rewards available because of your current struggles? What good can come out of this season of life? Where can you minimize any losses? Where can you open doors wider for greater blessings?

> *Lord, nothing needs to be wasted. You can take all of me and my days and do something extraordinary. You bring me greater returns than I ever knew possible. Even in my heartaches and losses, You will help me plan a strategy to minimize loss and increase spiritual reward. Thank You!*

Trusting God Through the Pain

Trust in the LORD with all your heart and lean not on your own understanding.

PROVERBS 3:5

I'm a mom of three young children. I love them more than I can say, but some days they would say I don't love them very much. I make decisions that anger them, sadden them, and sometimes frustrate them. I love them enough to make these decisions because I'm looking out for their best interests.

I recently had to make a tough decision that brought great sorrow to their hearts. We had adopted a large, mixed-breed puppy from a shelter. I've raised big dogs for nearly 30 years, and I am careful to train and condition each dog. But one night, in a horrible, unexpected turn, the dog jumped up and attacked my youngest daughter. I knew immediately I had to put the dog down. My kids wailed in sadness when I told them he wouldn't be at home when they got off the bus the next day. As an experienced big dog owner, I know aggressiveness in some dogs can't be corrected through training. And as a mom

I knew that no animal who attacks a child can be permitted to stay in our home or neighborhood. I loved my children too much to avoid the pain of putting their dog down.

If you could see my life and had to judge my love for my children by what I did on other nights, I wonder what you would conclude. When I call my children home at night, do I love them any less than those evenings when I let them stay out and play? When I tell my kids they may stay up and read, do I love them more than when I say "Lights out"? My love for them never changes, even when my decisions don't *seem* loving.

God's love doesn't change either. He loves you as much in this moment as He ever has or ever will. We may not feel loved when He says no to our prayers or gives others what we want for ourselves. God may never give you the weight, shape, or looks you desire. You may struggle with certain issues all your life. I don't understand it all, but I don't have to. And neither do you. You can turn to your Lord for courage and trust in His constant, unchanging love.

Lord, make my faith in You greater than my feelings about decisions I'm not pleased with. Grow my trust in You, and help me understand Your unfailing, all-encompassing love for me. Your love is greater than any situation or heartache that comes my way.

Godly Pleasures

You have made known to me the path of life;
you will fill me with joy in your presence,
with eternal pleasures at your right hand.

PSALM 16:11

We were created, in part, to experience eternal pleasures. "Pleasure" is a word we don't hear often, especially in church. How many sermons can you name that have highlighted the importance of enjoying ourselves in our spiritual lives? Perhaps it's because we've let the fallen world define pleasure. We think it has to have a hint of sin in it or it wouldn't really qualify, right? We've been deceived into associating pleasure and sin, when in reality no part of sin can be part of *true* pleasure. Pleasure is God's idea and His good creation. He designed us to experience good feelings. When we die and are welcomed into His presence, I'm sure there are many joys waiting for us.

But what about today? Can we find delights that aren't associated with sin in any way? Yes! Can we find God in earthly pleasures? I think we can. Why not try an experiment today? Eat as slowly as you can. Taste each and every bite. Concentrate on the experience of eating and the associated feelings. Too many of us claim we eat for comfort, when the truth is we eat for numbness. We eat so we will stop feeling. But what happens when eating becomes pleasure and is enjoyed slowly and with great intention?

Scientifically, I can tell you that your cravings will be reduced and you will remain full for longer even if you eat less. Spiritually, I can assure you that you will experience food as a gift from God—and a deeply pleasurably one at that. Slowing down today is an experiment in pleasure and in trusting that God's gifts are indeed good. Allowing yourself to experience joy might become one way you can bring balance back into your life.

Lord, I know You want me to know pleasures. But I'm afraid I can't experience something so good without it becoming sin. Help me understand that rejecting Your blessings opens the door for sin because then I crave satisfaction and joy. Help me slow down and seek pleasure within Your boundaries.

God's Answer Is Love

Hear my voice in accordance with your love.
PSALM 119:149

God's love is His most defining attribute. We sing about it, we write about it, we tell others about it. But do we really believe in it? And do we believe God believes in it?

When you pray, how do you think God decides on His answer? What is His guiding logic, the overriding principle He uses to choose what to do regarding you and your life? It's love. God's love forms the basis of *every* decision He makes on your behalf. He always answers your prayers with love toward you in His heart.

So many times we're ashamed to tell God what we really want or what we think we need. We worry we'll sound shallow, weak, or vain. And perhaps we will. It doesn't matter. God loves us and wants to hear from us. He wants our honesty. And He will answer *every* prayer with love. When we believe this, we will find the courage to pray according to today's verse: "Hear my voice in accordance with your love, God. Hear my desires, find my deepest needs, and answer me in the most loving way possible."

Then we begin to live a surrendered life, trusting that

every decision from the Lord is based on His love for us. We can be ourselves in the presence of Christ because we know that He understands us completely.

Whatever your struggle is today, whether weight, beauty, work, children, or romance, tell God about it. Invite Him into every aspect of your life and heart. The answer you will receive from Him is wrapped in His love—a love that redeems, transforms, blesses, nourishes, and leads to abundant life.

> *Lord, answer my prayers today with Your love. I know You will choose the most loving response. I trust You with my desires, failings, longings, and hopes. I am so thirsty for Your love. Pour it over me!*

Slowing Down

The LORD will guide you always; he
will satisfy your needs in a sun-scorched
land and will strengthen your frame. You
will be like a well-watered garden, like
a spring whose waters never fail.

ISAIAH 58:11

When I was younger, I knew a girl desperate for acceptance and love. To say she was promiscuous would be an understatement. She was sleeping with so many young men I quickly lost count. She was beautiful, and she had big dreams for her future. Our friendship only lasted for a season, and I went on with my life and career. A few years later, my friend did become a superstar in her business. Suddenly she was signing endorsement deals, getting invitations to appear all over the country, and earning millions of dollars. People waited in line to get her autograph and shake her hand.

And then it happened. Although she had the world's love and acceptance, she became embroiled in a sex scandal. Her career ended immediately. No more money; no more fame. She'd had everything she'd asked for, but perhaps nothing she wanted. She had beauty, the world's love and acceptance, fame, and money, but the hunger inside didn't appear to have subsided. Even with everything she wanted, life must not have been satisfying.

I wish we were still friends. I would tell her what I know now: The world can't satisfy any of us for long. We really don't want the world or its gifts. We hunger for relationship with God. We want a safe place to hide when we're scared and strong arms to hold us when we're weak. We want a loving heavenly Father to tell us we're beautiful. We want Him to let us know we're lovely and loved just as we are and that He will take good care of us. We want His love to give us what earthly beauty and acceptance cannot: a secure heart at peace.

> *Lord, sometimes I run after what can't help or heal. Shower me with Your goodness and mercy. When I start to turn to someone or something else for happiness, remind me who You are and how much I can trust You. Keep me from foolish decisions and selfish appetites.*

God Loves "Different"

He was despised and rejected by men,
a man of sorrows, and familiar with suffering.

ISAIAH 53:3

I watched a documentary about a beautiful (and slender) reporter who dressed in a special-effects "fat suit" to walk around a city and chronicle the responses and reactions she got from bystanders. No one was especially kind, and many were especially cruel. I got a little taste of this once too. When I was a young actress, I got a role playing a girl with a noticeable handicap. I worked with a specialist to learn how to walk and move as if I had a mild brain dysfunction and was physically handicapped. To test my skills, I went to a mall in a nearby suburb where people with very comfortable incomes lived. No one would look me in the eye. Salespeople spoke loudly and slowed their speech, as if I were deaf and couldn't understand their words. When I walked through a crowd, people stepped away from me. It was one of the loneliest afternoons of my life. This world is not kind to anyone who is different. The decision to show up every day and live life when you "don't fit the norm" is an act of courage.

You may be different. You may be "bigger than" or "smaller than." You might be "taller than" or "shorter than." You might have physical challenges or heavy emotional baggage. People who are different know one thing especially well: They are not eagerly welcomed in a world that worships perfection. Friend, you are not alone. You are adored, watched over, and protected. I pray that you will discover and experience these truths and allow them to soak deeply into your spirit, bringing you hope and healing in Christ Jesus.

Lord, You love "different." You aren't afraid or shy around those who struggle or stand out. You know what it's like to not fit in and be treated badly. Thank You for breaking the power of shame and defeat forever on the cross. Because You endured Your pain, I am free.

A Heart of Wisdom

*Teach us to number our days aright, that
we may gain a heart of wisdom.*

PSALM 90:12

Name three things you want people to say about you at your funeral. Here are my top three:

- She loved unconditionally.
- She was generous with her time and money.
- She showed me Jesus.

I also suspect a few people will say things like "I told her not to jump out of that plane at her age!"

Did you notice anything absent from my list? That's right. I didn't mention beauty in any physical form. We want to be remembered when we're gone for our character and heart. So why do we care so much right now what we look like? Our appearance will likely not be our enduring legacy. Beauty doesn't get us any closer to our goals and dreams that are based on God's standards and priorities.

Being worried about our weight, skin, hair, wrinkles, and such can distract us from pursuing our true purpose. God wants us to feel comfortable in our own skin so that our minds and energies can be focused on Him and the wild, wonderful adventures He calls us to. Making peace with our appearance is spiritually important because it frees us to embrace God's vision for our lives. I don't want to get to heaven and realize I wasted moments to serve and represent God because I was too busy worrying about my physical imperfections.

Life is short, and we don't know how long we have on this earth. We need to be wise and not allow our God-given opportunities to be wasted. Excess worry, obsession, and shame over what we can't control, including beauty, can drive us off course from experiencing the true beauty of life: fulfilling our destinies and roles in God's epic love story.

Lord, please give me a heart of wisdom so I will see beauty from Your perspective. I want to be wise with the days You've allotted me. Show me where and how I am wasting my time and energy.

Perfect for His Plan

The secret things belong to the LORD our God.

DEUTERONOMY 29:29

Did you know that a potato has more chromosomes than you do? For all our primping and posturing, we ultimately must come to the conclusion that we did not originate life. We did not design or plan our bodies. And while we have great influence over them now, we don't have much control over them. We are not the masters of the universe, even though we might aspire to be.

If such great care went into the creation of a spud, we can certainly appreciate that God has bigger plans, bigger purposes, and greater control over every aspect of our bodies than we understand now. Why not relax and relinquish control to Him? He loves you and will take care of you. He knows what His plans are for you. And this will help us welcome a little more humility into our perspective. We will never be perfect, but God says He can use us for His plans. We may never hit our goal weight or have the button nose we'd like, but we didn't get a say in our chromosomes, genes, lineage, or coloring. We are who we are by the grace of God. Whether God made another woman "more beautiful" than us isn't our concern. Besides, we know the truth now. He gave the lowly potato more chromosomes than a supermodel.

Lord, sometimes I laugh when I think of all the mysteries around me—the hints of another realm and greater truths. I am humbled to be called Your beloved daughter. I know that someday You will delight in revealing Your mysteries. I will know why You made me just as I am. Thank You for Your grace today.

Breaking Bad Habits

It is for freedom that Christ has set us free.
Stand firm, then, and do not let yourselves be
burdened again by a yoke of slavery.

GALATIANS 5:1

Are you being controlled by a bad habit? I know this struggle well. I eat too many sweets. When I'm training for a triathlon, I've been known to come home and eat lots of chocolate. I've also tend to cuss when surprised or frustrated. I once left an inspiring meeting at a world-famous evangelist's headquarters, got into the car, missed a turn, and verbally exploded. What a contrast to what I'd just experienced in the meeting! There seems to be no end to sin and bad habits in my life. No matter what I project on the outside, within me I'm struggling. Thankfully I'm always growing in Christ too.

If you too are dealing with a particular habit, stronghold, or pattern that doesn't seem to end or even improve, why not try the ancient spiritual practice of fasting? Fasting is generally defined as going without food for a set period of time to humble ourselves before God. You may choose to fast for one meal, one afternoon, or one day. When you feel the pain of sacrifice and discipline, use this as a prompting to pray. Give God your recurring struggles. Lift up others who are in pain and struggling too.

While fasting is my least favorite spiritual discipline, it has yielded some sweet, shocking miracles in my life. I've seen God heal and bless fellow strugglers, and in His gracious mercy, He has also broken the power of many recurring sins in my life.

Difficult struggles might be a call to develop spiritual discipline. If you think your spiritual life and inner woman needs a little extra help getting through a problem, hang-up, or habit, consider fasting a tool to try. God wants you to live a life of abundance. It's a spiritual paradox that giving up something often makes more room for this abundant life.

May God bless you as you humble yourself before Him and allow Him to work in your deepest struggles.

Lord, I want to humble myself before You. Make room in my heart and body for Your abundant grace and revelation. My struggles are so difficult and persistent that I wonder if I'll ever be free. Help me better understand the freedom I have in You and how that can translate into freedom from sin and bad habits.

The Power of the Process

*Whoever has will be given more, and he will
have an abundance. Whoever does not have,
even what he has will be taken from him.*

MATTHEW 13:12

If I had a magic wand, what would you rather have
today: successful results or a successful process? I have
grown to love and appreciate the power of process. I would
rather have a successful process in place than specific results.
When a process works, results are the natural by-product,
which is certainly one of the goals. But another primary goal
is to have the process go on. That way success continues. I
think this is why so many self-improvement efforts die off so
early. We give much thought to the result we want, but it's the
process that has the power to make or break our goal. If we
don't emphasize the process more than the result, we might
not achieve or be able to continue the positive results.

In the past, eating fruits and vegetables was only a means
to an end for me. I wanted to be thin, so I ate "rabbit food."
Two things happened fairly quickly: I either lost weight and
then went back to eating my favorite junk foods or I got discouraged over the lack of results and went back to eating my

favorite junk foods. Either way, junk food won. I didn't want to eat healthy for the sake of eating healthy. I wanted to eat healthy to be thin. I wanted the results, not the process.

Thankfully, God is patient. I began to understand that the process was more important than the immediate result. I let go of my demands for a thin, perfect body. I began eating healthy foods because it was good stewardship of the body God gave me. I wanted to eat in a way that kept my body healthy regardless of whether I got thin or not. I eventually grew to love the process and gave up worrying about results.

You probably won't be surprised to learn that my weight has been stable for years now. While it's not runway-perfect, it's just right for me. I have peace because I embraced the process.

Lord, it's easier to want the results rather than process some days. The process often requires hard work, sacrifice, and persistence. Thank You for Your patience and gracious leading. Lead me to mentors and wise counselors who will show me better ways to live and serve You.

Thinking v. Doing

*Let us not become weary
in doing good, for at the proper time
we will reap a harvest
if we do not give up.*

GALATIANS 6:9

We can't always think our way into feeling better. Sometimes we have to act our way into it. Actions can often change feelings immediately. For instance, if you struggle with poor self-image, you are probably engaging in behaviors that make you feel bad about yourself, such as overeating, gossiping, and avoiding relationships. Women who exercise and eat healthy foods report higher satisfaction with their bodies no matter what their weight or size. Let's think about that for a moment. A woman who is morbidly obese but chooses to eat her vegetables and get a walk in before dinner might feel better about her body than a super-model who skips lunch to fit into a bikini.

What we do matters, and not just because we want results. What we do informs the people around us how we feel. How we feel, in turn, influences what we do. One positive action can reap a harvest of good feelings, that lead to more good actions, that lead to even more good results. This cycle of goodness can repeat indefinitely.

Too often, though, we wait until we feel like changing before taking action. We want to "feel something" before we "do something." The trouble with feelings is that they can act like a stubborn cat. They won't come when called; they're furtive, unpredictable, and immune to our pleas. As my husband and I have learned, sometimes the only way to catch a cat is to feed it. We have been known to rig a long extension cord to a can opener and drag it outside. When our cat hears the can opener, he knows supper is on the way and comes running! We have learned to take action.

So it is with us. When we're held hostage by emotions that won't change, we have to take action and trust that the feelings will sort themselves out later.

Lord, it's hard to take a step in the right direction when I'm feeling negative. It's like being caught in quicksand. But You tell me if I reach out to You—if I take action—the quicksand will release me. Give me the courage to act and the patience to wait for the feelings to catch up.

God Speaks Your Language

*You have granted him the desire of his heart and
have not withheld the request of his lips.*

PSALM 21:2

How many languages do you think God speaks? I believe He can speak every language ever invented and a few we don't know about. I also know God speaks in individual dialects. For instance, I'm a dog lover. I know God "speaks dog" to me because He has so often revealed His gracious love through my work with canines. I know friends who are mathematical whizzes, and I hear them marvel at God's love of order and precision. God must "speak math" to them.

Scientists find God in the laboratory, mountain climbers find Him on rugged peaks, and mothers find Him in the nursery. Whatever we love, God speaks that language. He will use whatever we are drawn to as a way to reveal Himself and invite us into a deeper walk with Him.

That's why I'm so excited about writing this book to share with you about true beauty. We live in a culture obsessed with appearance. It's only natural that some of this affects us, and that we'll wonder how much physical beauty matters in a spiritual woman's life. We might even feel a bit guilty if we want to be more beautiful.

Who can we talk to about this? God speaks beauty! The Creator of all color, the Maker of all women, the Master of proportion and balance and contrast is available to us. He not only has exquisite taste and impeccable artistry, He can use all the confusing longings in our hearts as open doors to bring more love into our lives. Because God speaks all our languages, He knows how to use our frailties and foibles to show us who we truly are in Him. We are the beloved, beautiful daughters of a majestic King.

Lord, You are the only true, living, loving God. Thank You for using my passions and faults to draw me closer to You. You shower me with ever-increasing blessings. Help me reveal to the people around me how much you want to communicate with them.

God, the Architect and Builder

For the LORD God is a sun and shield;
the LORD bestows favor and honor;
no good thing does he withhold
from those whose walk is blameless.

PSALM 84:11

Your body is composed of 3 billion chemical building blocks laid out in particular sequences that create your personal DNA. That's just slightly less than the number of people who own cell phones in the world. If you can, imagine lining up everyone in the world with a cell phone, in an exact order, at exactly the same moment. That's the incredible detail God used to create you!

God works on a very large scale, but He also controls the most minute details. He can assemble 3 billion building blocks in the right order. He remembers where each one is and why He put it there. He knows everything about you: your DNA sequence and why He gave you that one, your choice of salty versus sweet, spring versus fall, flip-flops versus high heels. He has known every one of your ancestors, and He can recite your family line all the way back to Adam and Eve. When your relatives were fighting to survive through the great medieval plagues, God was there. When they were crossing oceans to come to America, He was there. When you were growing in the dark seclusion of your mother's womb, He was there.

Yes, God is this big. This detail-oriented Being planned you and your appearance. Is there anything He could have overlooked or left out? No! Everything about you, inside and out, was crafted for His delightful purposes. Will He ever fail to bring you everything you need to fulfill His purposes? No! If you feel like you lack something, it's evidence of greater blessings to come and a purpose of His that hasn't come to fruition yet. He will bless you, bring you love, and call you to love others just as you are.

Lord, I believe You paid infinite attention to every detail of my creation. You are my sun, my source of light and life. You are my shield, my source of protection and comfort in battle. I accept everything about Your plan for my life: my design, my purpose, Your will for me, and Your blessings.

For His Glory

He gave him the plans of all that
the Spirit had put in his mind
for the courts of the temple of the LORD and all
the surrounding rooms, for the treasuries
of the temple of God and for the
treasuries for the dedicated things.

1 CHRONICLES 28:12

If you want to know how meticulous God is, read the biblical accounts of God's plans for His tabernacle and temple. Every measurement, color, accent, and elaborate decoration is dictated by God. The tabernacle, and later the temple, were God's choice of dwelling place among His people.

Please take a moment to reflect on these questions.

- Was God aware of what the finished structure would like look?

- Did He build it to please His tastes and plans, or did He let His people dictate what they wanted?

- Did He consult anyone for opinion or instruction?

- Did God approve of the final structure and dwell in it?

- Did He speak to His people from the sanctuary and perform miracles for them?

What blessed assurance and humbling truth! We are God's temple, built for His tastes and purposes—not our own. Within our mortal, failing bodies, God has chosen to dwell. We are designed to shelter a Spirit, and within this "Spirit house," God will meet with us and perform countless miracles on our behalf.

Lord, I am marvelously made, not for my glory, but for Yours. I was created not for my own popularity and prestige, but for Your purposes. May You use every failing and every flaw to draw me closer to You and point others to Your mercy and grace.

Letting Go, Letting God

*Do not worry about your life, what you will eat
or drink; or about your body, what you will wear.*

MATTHEW 6:25

"For every beautiful woman, someone, somewhere, is
tired of her." I read this on a bumper sticker once.
What a funny and true statement! John Ortberg titled one of
his books *Everybody's Normal Till You Get to Know Them*. Sim-
ilarly, some women are beautiful until you get to know them.
And some women who look quite ordinary become exquisite
once we know them well. And often, when we really get to
know someone, our opinion of him or her changes.

Physical beauty can't secure love. It can't even promise temporary affection. After all, every woman will appeal to someone, but no one woman appeals to everyone. We can't predict
tastes, and we can't control how people respond to us.

In my dating years, this frustrated me to no end. I learned
that some men preferred blondes or raven-haired beauties. It
didn't matter that I tried to make my redheaded self attractive. I was the wrong type. Some men preferred leggy women,
some didn't. I knew I would marry my dinner date when he
leaned over the table and said, "I like girls with big hips." I

called my mom that night! I had found the man who found everything about me attractive—even my generous proportions. Grandmothers used to tell their daughters, "There's a lid for every pot," and I had found mine. We're still together 15 years later, and he still finds my "figure flaws" to be his favorite features. Isn't God good?

Don't you worry about your body, your looks, your hair, or anything else. There is indeed a lid for every pot. God will give the right man a distinct appreciation for you, and if you dare, you can let go of all your preconceived notions of beauty. We can be women who get more beautiful the more people know us. That is indeed the true, lasting kind. It requires no creams and no surgeries. It will grow and grow through the years.

Lord, who knows beauty better than You? Make my inner beauty so radiant that it's what people remember about me. I pray that others will be attracted to me because they sense Your love within me. Your love will make me forever beautiful.

Freedom from Insecurity

*Teach me your way, O LORD; lead me
in a straight path because of my oppressors.*

PSALM 27:11

There's good news for those of us who feel insecure. God has a plan to use our insecurities, our rejections, our disappointments. He will use those shaming oppressors to lead us down a better path—the path to a fulfilling life and an introduction into the secret ways of God.

Perhaps you opened this book hoping to make peace with some aspect of your body, your eating habits, or your appearance. God has a plan to use that longing to lead you in a new direction for your life—a way filled with grace, mercy, joy, and freedom. The insecurities that have held you down for so long will be working *for* you instead of against you because they will remind you to turn to and cling to God.

Have you been resisting depending on God? It's human nature to want to make our own path and go our own way. Independence is a beloved virtue in our culture. Individuality is prized above obedience. But life without God is filled with oppression, and there is no remedy for that apart from God. Tyranny of any kind, including self-imposed or other-imposed criticisms, can drive us back to God. We can choose to willingly follow Him down new paths, to learn His ways and listen to His wisdom.

Please don't be bashful about approaching God with your insecurities and doubts regarding your beauty and appearance. He understands that we live in a culture obsessed with looks and physical attributes. He will be so tender with you, gentle and adoring with a plan to uplift you and turn those oppressors into opportunities to grow and bless you. God won't allow the pressures of the world to rob you of your riches in Christ and the blessings of walking alongside Him.

Lord, what marvelous grace You offer me! I can come to You with anything—any fear or oppressor, any desire or longing—and You will use it as an opportunity to teach me and lead me down the path to Your peace. Thank You.

Mind v. Will

Whoever loves discipline loves knowledge,
but he who hates correction is stupid.

PROVERBS 12:1

We live in an information age. Whatever you need to know, the facts are just a mouse-click away. We can know the nutritional content of foods, down to the last milligram of sodium and fat. We can know how food works inside our bodies to nourish or deplete us. We can know how much we need to eat to maintain our weight, lose weight, or gain weight. We can know just about everything we might possibly be interested in about food and eating. Unfortunately, we just don't know how to make ourselves consistently follow a healthy eating plan.

Why is there such a disconnect between knowing the right thing to do and doing it? Doesn't it seem like most of our problems are a result of this breakdown between the mind and the will? Knowing what to do is of little value if we don't follow through and get it done. The information age isn't exactly the pinnacle of human achievement we hoped it would be. Raw information hasn't changed human nature.

Today's verse hints that we might have the process backward.

First comes discipline, and then comes knowledge. Without discipline, we remain stupid, to use the Bible's not-so-gentle language. Information *is not* intelligence. Intelligence is practicing self-discipline.

The problem with discipline is that it hurts. It's painful, uncomfortable, and even scary at times. We have to alienate ourselves from our favorite habits. And new habits don't usually immediately feel good either. They feel foreign and awkward. But the Bible says if we love discipline, we love knowledge. We can become rare people in our information age—people who *act* on information instead of just absorbing it. We can become women of discipline and power.

Lord, I know what I need to do, I just don't always want to do it. Walk me through the painful moments of transformation. Ease me into the discipline to get things done. Create in me a hunger for the discipline that leads to a fuller and deeper life in You!

The Beauty Mask

*[Jesus] welcomed them and spoke to
them about the kingdom of God, and
healed those who needed healing.*

LUKE 9:11

I feel fat."

How many times have you heard or said those words? Many times we complain about our weight or appearance when that's really not what's weighing on our hearts and minds. Digging down to the truth of our condition, whether it's loneliness, frustration, a nagging dread of the future, or financial issues takes hard work. It requires time and effort.

So instead of doing the work to unearth the truth, we choose to grouse. We use our focus on beauty as a mask, pretending that if our appearance were perfect, our lives would be too. We obsess on beauty to avoid looking within and to prevent others from seeing who we truly are. Beauty becomes a scapegoat for everything we don't want to deal with. But just as no one can run on broken legs, we can't become beautiful until what is broken within us has been healed.

There is hope! Jesus welcomed those who sought Him, including women who needed His healing touch. He is the

Great Physician—and a specialist too. He is tender, wise, strong, and gentle. We have nothing to fear from Him, and He wants to show us how much He loves us.

I know you've been hurt, and that even now you are hurting. Beauty is sometimes a mask for you. If you're like me, you'd rather hate your thighs and complain about your skin than admit to the scarier truths about your life. Take courage! God loves you. When you talk to Him, He will reach in and heal you—if you let Him. Don't wait until you're perfect or even slightly improved before approaching Him. That might never happen on your own. Settle in at the feet of your Savior and Lord. Rest your weary head against Him, and let His love wash over you.

God, all of my life I've felt pressured to measure up. I know I'm anything but perfect, so I struggle to accept myself. Your Word says I am Your precious daughter and a beautiful expression of Your love. Grant me the courage to believe that.

Only Love Is Eternal

These three remain: faith, hope and love.
But the greatest of these is love.

1 Corinthians 13:13

When I first read this verse as a child, I felt sorry for faith and hope. It hardly seemed fair that God said love was the greatest. Years later I heard a minister explain. Faith and hope are not eternal. They won't last forever. Only love never ends. Only love will follow us into heaven. When we arrive at the gates of heaven, we will no longer need faith. The Bible says, "We shall see [God] as he is" (1 John 3:2). We will no longer need hope on that day because all of our hopes will be met, fulfilled, and confirmed in the presence of Jesus.

Love is constant. And I believe love defines heaven. We will be surrounded by those we love, and we will love God as we never could before, taking in all His perfection. We will know and experience the full measure of love. Perhaps this is why we'll get new bodies when we get to heaven. I'm not sure the human heart is capable of holding that much love. We'll need to be made new to comprehend all the blessings, comforts, joy, and deep love that will surround us.

The promise of heaven is a comfort and a challenge. Heaven

is a comfort because faith and hope can be such difficult work here on earth. In heaven we probably won't have to work this hard. And even if we do, it will be a joy because we'll be in the presence of our Savior! But for today we have to wrestle our emotions and earthly intellect if we want to hang on to hope and continue to walk in faith. We can persevere through these challenges knowing we won't always have to fight to attain our dreams. Heaven is a comfort to us on the hard days.

But heaven can be a challenge for the same reason. Only here on earth does God ask us to walk in faith and hope. Only here can we demonstrate to a lost world what faith and hope can do. Our time is limited, so we need to share the gospel and the love and hope we have in Christ while we can.

So, dear sister, let's not waste any time obsessing about appearance. Let's stop criticizing God's handiwork and doubting His goodness when He created us. Let's practice accepting ourselves and our unique appearance with faith and hope. On earth and in our lifetimes we are given the gift and tools called faith and hope. Let's embrace ourselves fully in both, believing God has been good to us and sharing the Good News!

God, today grant me greater faith, greater hope, and greater love. Give me the strength to exercise all three to the fullest of my ability. When I get weary, remind me that heaven is just around the corner. Help me have courage and endurance.

The Littlest Decisions

*Catch for us the foxes, the little foxes that ruin
the vineyards, our vineyards that are in bloom.*

SONG OF SONGS 2:15

Experts estimate that we make approximately 35,000 decisions every day. Even simple activities, such as eating and drinking, can total more than 200 individual decisions per day. It's astonishing to consider how small and how many decisions shape our daily lives. While we may struggle over making "big" decisions, science tells us plainly that it is the little decisions that shape our walk. We may choose what car to buy only once in ten years, but every moment of every hour we choose what to think about, what to say, and what to do.

These little decisions add up to a huge impact. If we aren't vigilant about the little choices, they can become like the "little foxes" in today's verse from Song of Songs. When a vineyard is in full bloom, the fruit is not far behind. Months of work are about to be rewarded in delicious abundance...as long as the foxes don't steal the harvest.

I so understand this! Last year I planted heirloom tomatoes in my garden. I tended the vines daily. Just as they began to bear fruit, the beautiful tomatoes fell off and rotted on the ground. All my work was ruined! Upon closer inspection, I saw teeth marks on each one. An animal had sneaked into my garden and ruined my harvest. All my work came to nothing despite my diligence and intentions. I did everything right except keep the little animals out.

What little foxes are you allowing into your garden today? Are you grumbling about your thighs, hair, or nails, all the while supposedly honoring God? Are you nibbling on junk food while asking God to help you live at peace with your body? These little decisions are unwelcome intruders into the vineyard of God's blessings for you. They will ruin the harvest if you let them in and, even worse, give them sustenance. Wise gardeners (and now me!) know that it's not enough to plant the right seeds, water faithfully, and fertilize on a regular basis. We have to protect the plants to get the harvest.

I encourage you to protect the harvest God has planned for you. Keep the little foxes out of the vineyard. Pay attention to the small decisions just like you do the large ones. Guard against joy stealers that can spoil happiness and even ruin outcomes. Decisions about what to eat or what to wear may not seem important, but they may open the door to little foxes sent in disguise to sabotage your spiritual growth.

Lord, I am often focused on the big picture, worried about "bigger" issues, and praying about the life-changing decisions I face. Yet some real dangers in life can come about by the small decisions I often overlook or make hastily. Help me protect the harvest of blessings You are planting within me and around me.

The Number of My Days

Show me, O LORD, my life's end and the number of my days; let me know how fleeting is my life.

PSALM 39:4

I attended a funeral today. My friend died in her thirties, leaving behind a grieving husband and two children. I knew she'd struggled with her figure for years, and that she always felt badly about never achieving a model's look. As hundreds of friends and family gathered to celebrate her life and say good-bye, not a word was said about her weight. We talked about her appearance, yes, but we commented on her eyes that sparkled with love and the smile that made everyone relax. My searing private grief gave way during the service to a deep, overwhelming compassion for all of us left behind. My friend had made external beauty and thinness a priority in her life, and this standard caused her much pain. In the end what mattered to everyone who loved her was her spirit and the beauty she brought to others and out in others.

I need to review this lesson often. Recently I competed in

a triathlon, and the race officials used a permanent marker to write our race numbers down one leg and our ages down the other. We were ranked not only according to our finish times but also per our age bracket. As I ran, I eagerly noticed everyone's age. Was I in better shape than the woman who was ten years younger than I? Was that 70-year-old ahead of me? As I ran, I felt a deep sense of conviction. I had no right, my inner voice seemed to say, of setting standards for myself that didn't come from God. He alone had the right to tell me what I was supposed to aspire to. I'd been running my entire life like this race, comparing myself to other women and holding myself to a standard of appearance that ultimately meant nothing.

When I die, no one will care what I weighed. No one will share stories of how I conquered my problem skin or how I overcame weak and splitting nails. All that will matter is whether I was loved and loved. Love is all we can truly leave to others, all that will matter on this earth. Let everything today be done for love, in love, and by God's love. These are the priorities we can aspire to with joy.

God, teach me how to number my days correctly and value my time on earth. I get so blue when the scale moves in the wrong direction, my skin breaks out, or I fall short of the world's standard of beauty. Remind me of the importance of love.

The Truth About Imperfection

*Not that I have already obtained all
this, or have already been made perfect,
but I press on to take hold of that for
which Christ Jesus took hold of me.*

PHILIPPIANS 3:12

One fear has always especially haunted me, and perhaps you too. I suspect that someone, somewhere, has a better life than I do. My "mystery woman" has a better body, more money, less housework, perfect children, a new car, and she can eat whatever she wants without gaining an ounce. Age and gravity have never disturbed her looks. I want her life.

I'm mad at this woman. I dislike her. I look around for her everywhere, but all I ever catch is a fleeting glimpse. No one I know has perfection in abundance. We all have little bits of it here and there, but no one has the whole package. If this is true, why do I always have a nagging suspicion that it exists somewhere? Perhaps because I was made in God's image and, therefore, destined for perfection.

We once had perfection…long ago in a garden called Eden. But we blew it. We were meant for perfection, but because of Adam and Eve (and the rest of humanity's sin), we're living imperfect lives. This nagging feeling of loss and envy is perhaps heaven-sickness in disguise. If the desire for perfection originated in God and was fulfilled by God, my longing for relief from imperfection is really more about my longing to be more like Him than an envy of others.

When I consider this truth, I can live at peace, knowing my ultimate desire will not be fulfilled here on earth but will be in heaven. This life-on-earth-centered desire stirs my spirit to seek God. It never lets me get too comfortable when times are good. The yearning makes me run faster to God when times get bad. And this desire brings me face-to-face with the truth of my chronic imperfections. Despite what advertisers promise, I won't be able to achieve permanent perfection. Something will always be off in my life, my body, and my world. I don't think this is fatalism; I think it's freedom. I release myself from the burden of chasing what isn't available on earth. I accept imperfection with a sigh and the sweet comfort that it will not last forever.

God, envy rots the bones and steals my joy. I know no one is perfect, but sometimes I think I see it in other women. In those moments, whisper in my ear, reminding me that I am Your daughter. Give me the grace to accept imperfections in me, in my life, and in others.

For Such a Time As This

*And who knows but that you have come to
royal position for such a time as this?*

ESTHER 4:14

Esther was a young orphan living in the care of an older relative. She had already survived the terrible heartache of losing both parents. Then King Xerxes of Persia forced her to join his harem. Once again Esther was torn from the life she knew. And she would never be able to return to life as she knew it. Whatever dreams she had as a young girl were broken forever.

And yet Esther persevered. She didn't turn bitter, rebellious, or angry. I'm sure she had moments of those emotions, but she didn't allow them to take root and grow. We know from Scripture that she persevered under the care of the harem overseers and heeded their advice. She was willing to continue living in circumstances she would never have voluntarily chosen.

God works through people who stay the course even when the way turns rough and hostile. Our paths through life may feel uncomfortable, but that doesn't mean God is immune to our suffering. And we may feel inadequate, but God created each one of us for a special destiny. If Esther were sitting beside you right now, I'm sure she would tell you these truths. In fact, she might even remind you that she was given beauty to appeal to one man in particular: King Xerxes. Through him, Esther would save her people from destruction. God made Esther in such a way that she was best able to accomplish her destiny. And He has done the same for you.

My dear sister, no one can take your place. You were created for just this moment—for your life and for your specific loved ones. You were designed, head to toe, inside and out, to accomplish beautiful, divine purposes in this world. To believe anything less—to doubt your looks, your talents, your place in God's story—is to doubt God's intelligence.

My prayer for you today is that you will find the strength to continue on even when the going gets hard. No matter what you are facing today, no matter what you feel or fear, I pray you will find the strength to say, "I too may have been created for just such a time as this."

God, You alone know how my story will end, how all of these circumstances will work together for Your glory. You gave me this specific body, these specific looks, and my passions, abilities, and interests. Help me follow You and fulfill the plans You have for me.

When You're Afraid

The LORD is with me; I will not be afraid.

As a mother of three young children, I know bad dreams sometimes come in the night. And when I hear those little feet running down the hall to jump into my bed, I know that nothing I say will comfort my young ones completely. No matter how many times I promise that there are no monsters under their beds, my children will not stop being afraid. At those times, words are useless. All that truly comforts my frightened children is my (or my husband's) presence.

Adults have bad dreams too, and often our inner fears are like bad dreams we can't wake from. We fear we are not pretty enough, or thin enough, or successful enough. We worry about what we've become or what we'll never be. We fret that we don't have enough and never will. In those moments, we can't really hear what others have to say. Our fears are so real, so scary, so powerful that words are useless. We need the comforting presence of our compassionate, gentle heavenly Father. God loves for us to run to Him, nestle into His arms, and tell Him all about the scary monsters in our lives. He doesn't grow impatient with us or tell us to "get over it and grow up." God comforts us in our weakness and fears with His gentle, wise presence. And because He is all-powerful—the Creator of heavens, earth, and us—He alone can speak the words our spirits really need to hear. He knows what we need and what will dissolve our fears. When God speaks into our spirits, change happens. We are set free.

Today when your fears send you running for comfort, seek your Father in heaven. Open the pages of His Word and soak in His presence. Listen for His comforting wisdom and compassion. You don't have to be brave and face your fears alone. You don't have to pretend troubles don't exist, even if some problems seem small or embarrassing. It's okay to be a frightened daughter who needs her Creator Dad. Jesus loves you dearly, and He wants to wrap you in His arms and hold you safely throughout the night. Everything will be all right.

> *God, I'm afraid. My fears are so real, so big, so scary! I feel like I should be stronger than this, but the truth is that I need You, Abba Father. I need to feel safe, protected, and cherished. Speak Your words of freedom and truth until I am free of fear. You are my comforter extraordinaire. Thank You!*

Disappointed

*Hope does not disappoint us, because God
has poured out his love into our hearts by
the Holy Spirit, whom he has given us.*

ROMANS 5:5

In this life we have plenty of disappointment. Perhaps we didn't get the body we wanted, or the looks, or the talent. Or maybe we didn't get the job we wanted, or a huge inheritance, or any number of wonderful things. We so easily grow discouraged and angry at God. Why does He allow us to desire something and then keep it out of our reach? How can He be good if He doesn't give us what we want or think we need? And if He has no intention of giving us what we want, why won't He remove our desire? Our ability to hope seems like a curse at times.

Hope is, at its essence, a hunger for God. We hope because we are earthly creatures who were meant for a different existence. Hope is a sign that we are precious in God's sight. It keeps us looking for what is bigger and better than what we have now.

Children of God have the brightest hope because we know we have a future that will outshine anything we can imagine. And yet we also hope for the wrong things. We get distracted by wanting material blessings. We confuse earthly satisfactions with God's blessings. We can place great hope in God meeting our desires, only to discover that God's plan for our lives is not the same as ours. Our hopes may be shattered, but it doesn't take long for hope to grow again.

We are blessed even when our desires are thwarted. We are God's beloved daughters even when His answer to our petitions and prayers is no. We are created to continue in hope even when we worry that our desires may not be the same as God's plans. We can place our hope not in the outcome of our prayers and petitions, and not in the satisfaction of our desires, but in God's all-consuming love. This is the hope that "does not disappoint." When we are filled with God's love, shallow desires and wants fade. When we are wrapped in His loving presence, we realize we have everything we need for happiness, and nothing the world can offer matters. God's love consumes our lesser desires, even while it spurs greater hopes.

God will never refuse to pour out His love upon us and through us when we choose to believe in His Son and our Savior, Jesus Christ. Every request we make of God is answered through His love. Every desire we experience is an opportunity for God to reveal His love to us. We don't have to worry that our earthly hopes seem petty or insignificant. God may not grant them exactly as we request, but He will pull us into His embrace and pour out His love on us.

God, it's maddening to want something and not get it. Sometimes I wish You'd remove the desires from my heart that You don't plan on granting. And yet You are a mysterious God. You use my desires and hopes to draw me to You, and hope in You never disappoints.

Fooled by Beauty

*Charm is deceptive, and beauty is fleeting; but
a woman who fears the LORD is to be praised.*

PROVERBS 31:30

I just heard the news that one of the world's successful lingerie models committed suicide. I am grieved
to hear that anyone felt so hopeless, so alone, that suicide was
her final choice. And the awful news is a sobering reminder.
How many times have I rolled my eyes when a woman with a
perfect body and face tried to share her struggles? *What problems could she have?* I'd grouse. *She's perfect!* And yet I know in
my heart she's not because she's human like I am.

Because beauty is worshipped in our culture, we tend
to have strong reactions to women who *appear* perfect. We
don't always want to hear their struggles, and we don't always
want to celebrate their victories. Their beauty is an invisible
wall separating us. We're afraid that if we get too close, we'll
feel inadequate. Perhaps they are afraid that if they try to be
themselves, no one will accept them. So they seek the comfort and companionship of those who don't always have their
best interests at heart.

We have a responsibility to our sisters, and God never

made this responsibility conditional. He never told us we could avoid loving the women who bring out our insecurities. We are called to accept every person in all his or her faults and perfections and in all our faults and perfections. Accepting another woman means we open our heart to affirm her even if she seems so perfect she couldn't possibly need us. Women all around us are hurting—even the world's "most beautiful." Beauty does not insulate women from pain and heartache. So as daughters of our loving God, let's make sure we give approval and encouragement to all women. Let us lift up and offer comfort even when the wounds aren't obvious. Let us offer love even when we don't see how much they need it.

God, charm is deceptive and beauty is indeed fleeting. I'm tempted to look away from beautiful women because they remind me of my insecurity and imperfections. But that's not the way Your love works. Give me Your eyes, Lord, and a Holy Spirit-empowered sensitivity so I can minister Your love to everyone.

What Lies Beneath

*Let us not become weary in doing
good, for at the proper time we will
reap a harvest if we do not give up.*

GALATIANS 6:9

I have three large garden plots. Every spring one of my principal pleasures is choosing the plants to grow in each one. I am deliberate in each selection, knowing these gardens will feed my family for months. After planting comes the many hours of watering, weeding, and fertilizing. To the untrained eye, it may look as though my time is wasted during this season. After all, I have nothing to show for it at first. No fruits or vegetables appear. But I don't pause for a moment, and I never consider stopping my efforts because I know what lies beneath the soil.

Life began in a garden, and many of God's lessons can be learned in one even today. Have you carefully considered what you have planted in your garden—in your spirit and heart? Have you been deliberate about choosing scripture verses to meditate on that will feed you for the months and years ahead? Do you supply yourself with good spiritual teaching and good spiritual leaders and mentors? If you do, you can expect an abundant harvest of peace, joy, and comfort!

Some women have no harvest at all. They invest in self-help programs, diets, and makeovers because they've never tasted the fruit called acceptance or invited Jesus into their hearts to experience His unconditional love. They are like farmers who water, weed, and fertilize—but forget to plant seeds. No matter how hard they work, no matter how passionate or how diligent they work, their lives will never bear fruit.

The seeds we plant will bear fruit in their time. They will sprout, ripen, be harvested, and eaten. Each blessing blossoms on its own timetable, according to its nature and God's plan.

God, You are so gracious! You allow me access to Your heart through Your Word and the ministry of Jesus. As I meditate on love and wisdom, let them sink deep into the fertile soil of my soul. As I grow in faith, help the fruit of Your love expand into an abundance of goodness I can share with others.

Cosmetic Surgery

I will maintain my love to him forever,
and my covenant with him will never fail.

PSALM 89:28

recently received a letter from a woman considering cosmetic surgery. She wanted to have the surgery but wasn't sure whether God would approve of such an expensive procedure done merely for appearances. A cosmetic surgeon I once interviewed for a story told me this dilemma isn't unusual. Her patients, she said, were often worried that if they had elective surgery God would be mad at them because they were changing the way He made them.

The first step, as I shared with the woman who wrote to me, was to seek wise, godly counsel. The second step was to make sure her finances were in order so she'd be generally prepared for unexpected needs that might arise. The third step is to consider the specifics of the surgery. If the surgery meets a physical need, I believe that since our God heals, He has provided ways for people to attain medical knowledge to correct physical defects or handicaps that prevent us from living a full, enjoyable life. I know of people who have had surgery because their facial lines made them look angry or weary all the time. These people worried that they were communicating negative messages to others. On the other hand, if the need you feel is basically emotional, surgery will never fully satisfy your perceived need.

After considering these issues, if you still want the surgery and are feeling conflicted, remember that you can wander away from God's will but you can never remove yourself from His love. No surgery will make God stop loving you! You cannot lose God's love, protection, and affection. He will keep loving forever. Pray about your decision, seek His answer, make the decision, and rest in the knowledge that you are loved no matter what.

God, there are many options available to me, and I struggle to know Your will. I want to be a good manager of all You've entrusted me with, including my health and financial resources. Please give me Your wisdom and surround me with godly friends I can turn to for wise advice. Speak to me through Your Word.

Beauty in Hard Times

*I will meditate on all your works and
consider all your mighty deeds.*

PSALM 77:12

When we're suffering, we hurt all over. We look in the mirror and see dark circles and new wrinkles. We find it difficult to get in touch with the beautiful women we were created to be. It's hard enough staying in touch with God when we're feeling good. When we get run down, exhausted, and ragged around the edges, we often let a lot of things fall by the wayside. What's a woman to do?

In those situations, especially when we see that our circumstances are not likely to change for a while, it's good to nurture the beauty within even if we don't feel it. A long bubble bath, a manicure, even a new fragrance can give us a little lift just when we need it. This is not being superficial. We're allowing God's earthly pleasures to minister to our feminine souls. And while we take a moment to care for ourselves, we can thank God for the beauty all around us and the beauty within us. Meditating on His beautiful goodness is balm for a wounded spirit.

The God who can create a flower out of a hard, brittle seed

can bring extraordinary beauty out of any of life's disasters. Beauty reminds us that where we begin is not where we'll end up. We don't see and can't comprehend all God can do. His creation reminds us that He can turn something ordinary or even ugly into something wonderful. God is at work, and He has unlimited resources! One of my favorite prayers when I'm faced with a long and difficult trial is to ask God to send me relationships. If I pray for my trial to end, I might have to keep praying for the same thing for months or even years. But I can ask God, who holds all believers next to His heart, to send me wise friends and counselors. And He always does! I find such comfort and beauty in the sweet words and encouragements these friends offer. Trials come to all of us, and all of us can find strength and support in God and each other.

God, roses are not immune from winter, or pests, or diseases, yet they are so beautiful when they bloom. And who would imagine that a tiny seed could turn into a breathtaking blossom? Even so is my life. What I see now can become something unimaginably beautiful under Your creative power.

Strength for the Battle

For this reason I kneel before the Father...
I pray that out of his glorious riches he may
strengthen you with power through
his Spirit in your inner being.

EPHESIANS 3:14,16

For this reason I too kneel before the Father. I am praying for you to be strengthened today through His Spirit. Whatever battles you face, whether a discouraging habit, a disabling fear, or a hostile environment, I am praying that God's Spirit will fill your inner being, leaving no room for thoughts of defeat and despair.

When we face battles, we need strength and comfort. We need to be filled up and made ready. If we don't seek the Spirit, we may try to satisfy our hunger or dull the pain by getting filled up at the refrigerator. Some go shopping and fill up their cars with bags. Some of us attack the only person we really have control over—ourselves. We beat ourselves up. We berate ourselves. We tell ourselves the problem is our looks, lack of skills, or ineptness. If we were thinner, curvier, prettier, glitzier, accessorized, tailored, elegant, alluring, smarter, more creative, more coordinated, we wouldn't have problems. And doing this creates even more trouble because we're basing decisions on false hopes and spending money we don't have, eating foods that aren't healthy, and acting out in ways that don't build us up or help. All this chaos distracts us from the pain of our problems, but nothing satisfies and gives victory—except God through His Holy Spirit.

God loves you just as you are. He is ready to fill you with His peace and strength the moment you ask. Even if you are halfway through a pie, on the way to the cash register, or whatever, if you ask He will reach you and give you peace so you can walk away from the self-defeating behaviors. He will remind you that problems existed in this world long before you got here, and even when you are busy adding your own troubles into the mix, He loves you and will see you through. He created you just as you need to be to accomplish His unique purposes. He won't give up on you, so don't give up on yourself.

God longs to fill you with His Spirit! Don't hesitate to come to Him on even when your spirit feels empty...or you've reached the bottom of the energy tank. There's hope! Let God fill you, satisfy you, and give you comfort.

Lord, I have trials and problems to face, and sometimes when I'm overwhelmed and empty, I let go and seek relief by blaming myself or turning to whatever is handy for comfort so I don't have to deal with things. But for lasting help and health, I need to turn to You. Give me the courage to accept myself as I am and the patience to wait for Your wisdom and guidance.

God's Unimaginable Power

Now to him who is able to do immeasurably
more than all we ask or imagine, according to his
power that is at work within us, to him be glory.

EPHESIANS 3:20-21

God is so generous. Perhaps you picked this book up hoping to get a boost to your self-esteem. God has so much more planned for you today! He wants you to feel His peace when you look in the mirror, yes, but He also wants to bless you and affirm His powerful, omnipotent love for you.

When we trust God enough to come to Him with our problems—large or small—He is excited. He loves being trusted with our concerns. He delights in answering them and helping us. He loves to respond to the deepest cries of our hearts with soothing solutions and comfort. God is so generous that when we ask for even a small consideration, He gives us more than we imagine possible. Scripture tells us our heavenly Father enjoys blessing us so much that we won't have room to hold it all. Imagine that! Imagine receiving an answer to every single prayer in your heart, and even more requests that you were only vaguely aware of. God will do all that and more because He loves you and you trusted Him enough to sit down and talk to Him about your feelings, emotions, desires, and needs.

You don't need to apologize or feel hesitant to approach God about beauty issues. He created you woman, and He understands your heart, spirit, and soul. Fully open your heart to Him and wait patiently for His guidance. Trust in His goodness and in His desire to bless you. Let go of what *you* think you should look like, or weigh, or have, or be. Ask God to help You become all He created you to be. Invite Him to glorify His name by the power He sets to work in your life.

May God's power sweep through every molecule of your body, every corner of your home, every second of your life. I pray that you will be so blessed that you can't wait to share what God is doing in your life with the people around you.

God, the thought of You blessing me like this is thrilling! You are able. You alone have the power. And to You will be the glory. Take all of me, Lord—all my heart, all my dreams, all my expectations, and all my desires. I choose to keep nothing back.

Keeping the Proper Proportions

I pray that you, being rooted and established in love, may have power, together with all the saints, to grasp how wide and long and high and deep is the love of Christ, and to know this love that surpasses knowledge—that you may be filled to the measure of all the fullness of God.

EPHESIANS 3:17-19

What do you really need today? I start each day in my office by making a list of what I need to get done. But what if I were to make a different list? What if I made a list of what I need? The truth is that I really have everything I need. I have shelter, food, and available medical care. I have loving relationships with family and friends. I have an omniscient, omnipotent, loving God. So why do I feel so needy, especially when I see beautiful women with perfect bodies on television or on the covers of magazines? What need am I trying to meet?

I believe a little voice inside me whispers that what I have isn't what I really need for happiness. "What you really need," this voice says, "is to be perfect. Everything you have means nothing if you're not one of the 'beautiful' people." There is a

A WOMAN'S PATH TO INNER BEAUTY

strong desire in me to focus on *my* wants and disregard all my needs that God has already met. Thankfully the love of Christ is a powerful antidote to the constant call to perfection!

By dwelling on and grasping (as much as possible) the enormity of Christ's love, everything else becomes small in comparison. And keeping this proper perspective and correct proportion are very crucial to staying afloat and moving forward. Speaking of proportion, I learned a very valuable lesson on one of my son's birthdays.

One year my son asked for a baby lizard. I considered his request and looked on the Internet to check it out. The picture of the critter was adorable. He was about an inch long and looked harmless. I ordered it. When it arrived, the "baby" was three feet long and would reach six feet at maturity. I'd not paid attention to proportions and made an incredibly foolish decision. The result? I had to turn our dining room into a "giant lizard habitat" until I finally found someone who knew this species of lizard and wanted it. We lived with the consequences of my decision for a long time. Had I stopped even for one minute to inquire about size, growth potential, and care for this beast, everything would have been different.

In light of this story, I encourage you to make your decisions based on the proper proportions and measurements. Ask how big God's love for you really is. I know you'll find that what you think you need, you already have. And what you still desire may fade away in light of His plans, desires, and love for you. In fact, you may find you need to adjust your prayers to fit His love instead of asking Him to adjust your circumstances.

Father in heaven, help me grasp how absolutely astounding Your love for me is. I need Your love that surpasses all knowledge and puts all I know and think into proper perspective. Show me how Your love dwarfs all my problems. Fill me with Your love so I don't have room for harsh self-judgments. May Your love be all I see everywhere I look!

Rescued from Shame and Fear

*A Samaritan, as he traveled, came where the
man was; and when he saw him, he took
pity on him. He went to him and bandaged
his wounds, pouring on oil and wine. Then
he put the man on his own donkey, took
him to an inn and took care of him.*

LUKE 10:33-34

What's stopping you from looking in the mirror and declaring, "God made me in His image, and I am beautiful!" I believe the reason why so many of us struggle saying these words has nothing to do with what we see in the mirror. The difficulty has nothing to do with our appearance, but rather with the space between our ears.

Our memories hold some painful secrets, don't they? We remember names we were called, negative comments that were made, and embarrassing moments when we knew we didn't measure up. Everyone else may have forgotten our awful moments, but we haven't. We remember and burn with shame. We're so afraid of being hurt again that we refuse to even dare call ourselves beautiful.

Shame and fear are enemies of beauty. They do not come

from God, who only leads us toward freedom and joy. So to embrace the path God wants for us, we have to deal with the robbers on this road, the thieves of freedom and joy. Shame and fear are those thugs. In the parable of the good Samaritan, a man is beaten and left for dead by thieves, and only one man dared to love enough to rescue him. My sister, you are the woman lying wounded in the road and Jesus Christ is the one man, the one God, who loves you enough to stop and rescue you. Though you have nothing to offer, though shame and fear have stolen precious years and trust, Jesus is stopping right now beside you, lifting you up from the dusty road, wiping away your tears, cradling you in His arms. He will carry you to safety and joy. All you have to do is let Him love you. Let Him bring you to a place of healing and to people He knows will love you in His name. Let Him wash your wounds and whisper sweet words of love and encouragement.

What thieves stole from you, He will replace with a treasure that can never be lost, taken, or destroyed—all-encompassing love. You are rescued and safe in His arms. You are loved. You are beautiful.

> *God, this world has left me wounded. Shame and fear have beaten me up. Rescue me, Lord. Move me to a place of healing. I want to feel Your love and know Your calm reassurance. Heal me, protect me, and show me who I am meant to be in You.*

Beauty Leads to Freedom

*It is for freedom that Christ has set us free.
Stand firm, then, and do not let yourselves be
burdened again by a yoke of slavery.*

GALATIANS 5:1

What does feeling beautiful mean to you? Is it being comfortable in your own skin, having a sense of gracefulness, or experiencing a deep sense of peace and well-being? Is it feeling deeply loved and appreciated? Each one of us has a unique "beauty signature"—a time or place that brings out our special beauty. I feel most beautiful after a long run. I jump into the shower covered in grime and dust from the road and smelling somewhat less than lovely, but as the hot water flows and I breathe deeply, I am so profoundly grateful for the gift of movement. I treasure the gift of my body at that moment without a single thought about its weight, form, or curves. I am grateful to *be*. There's nothing more I need to be and nothing I am ashamed of. I am fully present in my body, grateful for it, and at peace with it. That's my idea of beautiful.

What's yours? If you can't think of it easily, then I encourage you to practice being aware today. Look for those moments when your heart is at rest, when you are able to let go of your expectations regarding your appearance, when you find it easy (or at least easier) to accept yourself just as you are. Those are the times you want to look for and make room for in your life. Make a conscious effort to plan for the activities that bring you to this point. And in those time spans I believe God will speak to you and begin the deep healing work of mending your self-image and revealing to you what true freedom is all about.

When we find that place in our lives where we taste that tiny little bit of heaven on earth, when we can accept ourselves just as we are, without judgment or regrets, we will begin to crave this state of freedom in every area of our lives. We no longer want to spend our lives concentrating on the "shoulds": "I should lose weight," "I should have these wrinkles treated," "I should…" We sense that no amount of self-effort can take us to this wonderful and beautiful space.

God grants us this taste of beauty in everyday life to show us and lead us to the wide-open fields of His grace. This is what you were created for!

Jesus, show me where I most come alive to You and Your grace. Give me a hunger for Your way of life so that I won't be satisfied with any program of self-improvement or "should." I am made free by Your love, and I am made beautiful by Your touch.

God's Marriage Vows

*I am the LORD your God, who brought you
out of Egypt, out of the land of slavery. You
shall have no other gods before me. You
shall not make for yourself an idol in the
form of anything in heaven above or on
the earth beneath or in the waters below.*

EXODUS 20:2-4

Some biblical scholars believe the Ten Commandments
are best viewed as marriage vows. God is declaring His
love for His bride, the people of Israel, while also establishing
the boundaries of the marriage. The Ten Commandments
begin by God reminding the people that He alone delivered them from the slavery and oppression of Egypt. He
commands His bride to sweep away all other loves or gods
from her life.

No other god can provide for her or love her as the one
true God does. God's bride should enter into this sacred marriage with a commitment to forsake all others. Never again
should she look for provision, love, and protection from any
other god. Her God, her divine husband, will provide, protect, love, and cherish beyond all she can imagine or ask. But

before she can receive, she must choose to leave all others behind. Brides have a choice. They can choose who to marry and who to devote their lives, hearts, and bodies to.

Isaiah 62:5 reveals this same amazing love for you: "As a bridegroom rejoices over his bride, so will your God rejoice over you." God is committed to you, and He asks that you commit yourself to Him, body, heart, and soul. But you have a choice regarding who you run to for comfort, protection, affection, and affirmation. You can make beauty your god in hopes of earning love and attention. You can worship weight and idolize toned bodies and hope these will lead to fulfillment. Or you can acknowledge that the one God alone who created the heavens and earth has the power to fulfill you, to love you, to enable you to receive love that will last forever.

God will not force you into marriage. He will allow you to run back into the land of slavery and oppression. But even then He will wait for your return to Him. He is the knight in shining armor every woman longs for, the Prince of Peace who will love you without fail and without finding fault.

Make your choice today, my sister. Choose whom you will love. Choose the only God who will love you unconditionally and forever.

God, this world worships so many things. We worship bodies and wealth and beauty. Will You help me let go and turn to You instead? I choose Your love!

When You Want It, Give It Away

Share with God's people who are in need.

ROMANS 12:13

Throughout Scripture there is a unique principle at work. What we are tempted to hoard, God commands us to give away. Whether money or food, which were both forms of wealth, God consistently led His children to share what they most wanted to keep for themselves. In the same way, we are to share our wealth. Only then can we learn true freedom. Only then can the power of wealth be a blessing and not a curse. Finding the will to give money away means wealth won't have the power to take over our lives. Giving away what we value brings balance into our lives by requiring us to listen for God's voice and lean on Him. We will find freedom through sacrifice.

This same principle applies to other areas of life, especially in the area of physical beauty. In our world where beauty is coveted as much as wealth, few compliments are as prized as "You look lovely today" or "That color brings out your beautiful eyes." We long to be told we are beautiful. But to find lasting freedom, I believe God asks us to give away what we would most like to have for ourselves. This means making deliberate efforts to compliment, affirm, and encourage people. Why not wake up every morning determined to find the beauty in others and reflect it back to them? Become a woman who makes everyone feel beautiful, and you will find that you've never felt as free, lovely, or at peace yourself.

This principle unlocks another important spiritual door for us as well. When we affirm others, they feel safe with us. They are drawn to us. No matter what their spiritual condition, they seek our company and our words. Affirming and encouraging others gives us influence in their lives. This influence opens the door to speak truth to them, the life-giving eternal truth of Jesus, including His complete sacrifice, redemption, forgiveness, healing, and mercy. Through affirmation we open doors so others may choose to walk into the presence of Christ.

Our words have great power. They can help change how women see themselves. They change how women see us. And they can open the door for people to find their loving Savior!

Lord, You are so gracious and creative. By showing me how to see beauty in others, I am set free. Open doors so I can guide them to You. Give me Your eyes today so I can see true beauty in every woman and girl I meet. May I notice them and speak words that make them feel good about who You've created them to be.

Forever Loved

Give thanks to the LORD, for he is good;
his love endures forever.

1 Chronicles 16:34

One fact will never change: No matter how many days you live on this earth, you will *always* be loved. Love is the one constant in the lives of daughters of the most high God. Husbands may abandon us (by choice or by death) and children grow up and leave.

God and His great love, however, endures forever. His love embraces us even with all our imperfections, changes, and trials. We don't earn His love, but we can accept it. Knowing this, we are free to celebrate being in our bodies for the moment and living today as it unfolds. We don't have to try to hold on to love or coax it into staying. We will never take even one breath on this planet without being surrounded by God's love. His love never diminishes as we age, get wrinkled, gain weight, lose hair, and have diminished eyesight. God loves us for who we truly are—His precious daughters, His good creations.

Even so, sometimes we fear the changes we face. We're afraid that change means less love and more pain. If we let go of what we have, even a little bit, we might also lose the love we have. God promises that "goodness and love will follow [you] all the days of [your] life, and [you] will dwell in the house of the LORD forever" (Psalm 23:6). You will always have love no matter what else changes. Love is part of your identity. Love was the beginning of your story, and love will be your lasting destiny.

God, when I see so many aspects of my life changing, I worry about being loved less. I fear the world will pass me by, and I will be unloved and unvalued. But You have called me in love, and Your love endures forever. I will always wake up surrounded by Your love and go to sleep in Your love. Thank You!

Illuminated from Within

*Neither do people light a lamp and put it
under a bowl. Instead they put it on its stand,
and it gives light to everyone in the house.*

MATTHEW 5:15

A friend of mine is a stylist to the stars. What makes Michelle so special to her clients is her unique approach. She thinks of her clients as "Tiffany lamps." "What makes a Tiffany lamp beautiful," she points out, "is the illumination from within." The light shines through the glass creating a warm glow. Michelle doesn't try to "style" a client until she's discovered what makes the woman light up on the inside.

Some of us love God's creative artistry that is reflected in the natural world. We love flowers, fruits, waterfalls, and animals of all sorts. We enjoy fresh, crisp fragrances. Some women come alive when they read novels. They love the gift of story, of character, of the triumph of good versus evil, of the drama of life. Other women are artists. My mother and grandmother are both painters. They love color and pattern. Growing up, I remember my mother making me stop before every meal to notice and admire the colors on my plate. She thought green broccoli next to pink salmon was divine. And in a very real sense, she was right.

We all have the same source of illumination—God—but how He is expressed within us is different but always divine and deeply beautiful.

Knowing your unique passions will help you make choices that reflect your beauty to the world. Understanding how God wired you and what makes you feel alive will help you choose what clothes suit you best, the fragrances that inspire you, and the colors and textures to surround yourself with. Beauty becomes a celebration of God's illumination within you.

God gave you unique and powerful passions, and He finds joy when you express them. He wants your light to shine in this dark world to honor Him. So think about what inspires you and then share this with the people around you. Where you find beauty is also where God will lead the broken and lost of this world to find Him. Embrace what makes you unique. Hurting women need you!

Father in heaven, You created me with a unique design to best show off Your light in this dark world. I want Your light to fully shine through every part of my life. Let Your peace and love radiate through every part of my body, life, and spirit. Help me be an encouragement to people who are hiding or lost in the darkness.

Once upon a Time

The sun has one kind of splendor, the
moon another and the stars another; and
star differs from star in splendor.

1 Corinthians 15:41

Not so long ago, if a woman wanted a new dress, she
had to sew it herself or hire a seamstress. The seamstress
would measure her client's body and create a dress to fit the
woman. The woman's measurements dictated the dress's measurements. There was no such thing as a "standard size." However, when "ready made" dresses became available, women
had to fit the clothes. Clothes weren't made for each woman's
unique measurements.

Women soon began to identify themselves with a number—a size number. They compared their number with
other women's numbers. Women began to view their bodies as numbers in direct relationship to the other numbers.
And they began to fret over whether they could fit into the
clothes they wanted to buy.

Today, when a piece of clothing is manufactured, it is created to a specific set of measurements, and these measurements seem to rarely, if ever, be exactly ours. Each woman is

unique, but we are asked to buy standardized clothes. Please take a deep breath and relax for a minute as we take a look at clothing. Clothing manufacturers aren't designing custom garments. Few people will fit perfectly into off-the-rack, store-bought clothes. What are the odds that you will exactly match the size of the mannequins the manufacturers used to create the size?

So the next time you go shopping for clothes and few things seem to fit, I encourage you to remember that the problem isn't a body problem. The issue is mass production. Invest in a little tailoring to get the fit you want.

We've come full circle in a very odd way. We once called for the seamstress, and she produced the dress. Now someone produces the dress, and we call for a seamstress.

> Lord, it's a relief to know that not finding clothes that fit my body and size isn't a personal problem. You are a God of creativity, and You made each woman unique. Help me treasure everything that makes me one of a kind. Send me gentle reminders that I am beautiful just as I am, and I am not here to fit into someone else's mold.

In God's Garden

I am the true vine,
and my Father is the gardener.

John 15:1

In my garden I grow many varieties of flowers. I cultivate gardenias, magnolias, butterfly flowers, carnations, lantanas, lilies, lavender, sunflowers, moonflowers, coneflowers, and others I can't even name. Each flower is a treasure, and each one blooms according to its season and specific care needs. I look out for each flower in a specialized way, giving it exactly what it needs to flourish so that it will be healthy enough to look beautiful and withstand storms, disease, and pests. The magnolias require care that could kill my moonflowers. My petunias bloom best if I constantly pluck at the blooms, but my roses must be trimmed at the right place and at the right time.

I don't want the flowers to all look alike. That would break my heart and make my garden mundane and boring. I don't care to plant only one kind of flower either. Just as each is unique, each gets special care from me. I want my magnolias to be healthy and strong; I don't want them to become like my delicate lilies. All of my care and attention is designed to make the beautiful plants bloom and thrive. I want them to be everything they can be.

Like flowers, each of us is created uniquely. God didn't design us to be the same. He wants us to be the strongest, most vibrant version of ourselves as possible. His care and attention is designed to bring out the true essence of who we are, not to transform us into someone else. God is a great gardener who delights in providing what we need to bloom in dazzling displays of beauty, radiance, and sweet fragrance.

Aren't you glad God delights in a garden filled with variety, life, and vitality? I know I am!

Master Creator, You formed me to be a unique, breathtaking creation who can share Your goodness, mercy, and artistry with the people around me. When I am living in You, and all my energy and nourishment are rooted in You, my blooms truly radiate Your love. I praise You for not wanting me to be or look like anyone else.

The Shield of Faith

Take up the shield of faith,
with which you can extinguish all the
flaming arrows of the evil one.

Ephesians 6:16

*R*oman shields offered enormous protection in battle, covering a soldier from head to foot. The shields had special hooks on each side so that soldiers could hook their shields together to form a solid wall of protection. Facing heavy enemy fire, the soldiers could move forward as a unit, increasing their chances of success and survival.

In today's verse, God tells us that faith is our shield today. With this shield, we can move forward confidently, knowing we are protected from the attack of enemies—the "flaming arrows" of Satan and his minions.

So what were flaming arrows, and why did people use them? Flaming arrows delivered pain and destruction in two ways: they burned people by direct strike or set fire to structures and belongings that provided shelter and, often, the will to keep fighting. The arrow did damage, but the majority of the destruction was brought about by the fire. The best defense against these arrows were strong shields that the arrows would bounce off of and fall harmlessly to the ground to burn out.

In today's world we don't march into battle with old-fashioned shields and weapons like long, long ago. But the Bible tells us we are indeed in a battle daily. We are instructed to wear our armor every day and carry our shields so we can thwart the flaming arrows launched in our direction. Often today the enemy's arrows are destructive thoughts designed to take our focus off our Creator. "You ate too much!" "You will never be as pretty as your sister." "You aren't measuring up." If we allow these thoughts to have prolonged, direct contact with our minds, bonfires will burn out of control and consume our assurance of who we are in Christ and weaken our testimony of His love and provision.

You are not responsible for the flaming arrows launched in your direction; your responsibility is to lift your shield of faith in times of attack. And when you feel weak, when you are struggling to resist an enemy attack, remember that your shield is designed to connect to another believer's shield. Ask for help, for prayer, for companionship! You are not alone. Ask someone to come alongside you in the battle. And remember: You cannot be defeated! The King of kings and Lord of lords is on your side.

Mighty God, help me recognize the flaming arrows the enemy is shooting in my direction. Show me when to raise my shield of faith to extinguish the threat. Sometimes the enemy is devious, and those flaming arrows of destructive thoughts sound like my own voice. Give me discernment and guidance so I will recognize when the enemy is attacking. Give me the courage and strength to ask for help when I begin to falter.

Chosen

*In him we were also chosen, having been
predestined according to the plan of him
who works out everything in conformity
with the purpose of his will, in order that
we, who were the first to hope in Christ,
might be for the praise of his glory.*

EPHESIANS 1:11-12

Suppose I offered to take you into your favorite store
and buy you anything you want. You can only choose
one thing, but I will pay for it no matter how high the cost.

How much time would you spend in that store? How
careful would you be as you made your choice? Would your
choice reflect your tastes, your desires, your personality? I am
sure it would! I would love to know what your choice would
be because it would give me insights into who you are and
what you value in your heart.

Did you know God chose you in much the same way?
He had unlimited choices in your creation. He could have
added anything, in any combination, at any time. Out of
this wealth of possibilities, God chose to create you just as
you are. He picked your exact body type, weight, hair, skin,

and eye color. He selected your family and influences who your friends are and everything around you.

With His unlimited choices, He created you as a unique, one-of-a-kind daughter.

Have you considered that you reflect God's taste? God's personality? God's heart? God chose you for the praise of His glory and a testament to His goodness.

When I meditate on this precious truth—that I am chosen—I stand up straighter. I smooth out my hair and smile. I carry myself with dignity, and I treat others with respect. *You and I are chosen!* We made the "divine cut," so to speak. God created us perfectly for this time and place. He even paid the highest price imaginable for us—the blood of His own Son, Jesus.

There is no woman more honored, more valued, more beautiful to God than you are. There is no woman He loves more or prefers over you. God has made His choice—and you are His woman.

Father, I'm filled with awe to think You could have created anyone to fill my shoes, my place in time, but You chose me. Out of all the possibilities that were open before You, You wanted me. Help me meditate on this truth often today so I will reflect the joy and honor of being chosen by You.

An Abundant Life

The thief comes only to steal and kill and destroy;
I have come that they may have life,
and have it to the full.

JOHN 10:10

*G*od knows our desire to be beautiful. Throughout
Scripture He never tells us that wanting this is a sin.
He doesn't command us to abandon it always and
entirely. Rather, God intends to fulfill this desire in us completely. But His vision goes beyond what the world teaches
us about beauty.

Worldly beauty is about *getting:* getting acceptance, love,
and affirmation. In this view of beauty, there seems to be
a shortage of assets, and only "the pretty people" will get
them. Because of that, we're told we need to work hard to
earn them, making beauty entwined with fear and anxiety.
We dread swimsuit season, cameras, and activities that put
us in the spotlight because we're afraid we don't measure up.
We shy away from living life to the fullest even as we worry
that we're missing out.

Beauty in God's eyes, however, is about *giving:* giving
acceptance, love, and affirmation. And unlike worldly beauty,

the more you give, the more you have available to share! God wants you to experience true beauty and live life fully. When you trust Jesus with your life, including your looks, He will fill your life with joy, peace, and love. Yes, you'll still experience difficulties, but you'll discover abundant reasons to praise Him. His blessings will follow you all your days on earth and into eternity with Him.

As God allows each of us to experience His beauty, His intention is for us to pass His love and comfort on to others. Self-centered beauty tells us never to look at anything besides a mirror. God-centered beauty leads us to find peace in Him, and then encourages us to look beyond ourselves to help other people who need love and support. As we give, God replenishes and refills.

We serve a God of abundance, who gives beyond measure to each and every woman who seeks Him. Beautiful.

Father God, I have everything I need in You. When I feel less than beautiful, I know that is a sure sign I'm not seeking my beauty in You. Thank You for leading me in those moments to You so I can experience true beauty. And thank You for the many opportunities to pass on the love and hope You give me.

A Glorious New Creation

If anyone is in Christ, he is a new creation;
the old has gone, the new has come!

2 CORINTHIANS 5:17

God does not promise that you *can* be a new creation. He states you *are* a new creation. The work is finished. "But," you might ask, "how can that be? I still struggle with the same habits, temptations, and insecurities." If you are a new creation, why do you still feel like the same old you?

When you accepted Christ as your Savior and Lord, He changed you completely. You were given new life within. Think of an infant. Everything this infant will become height, weight, eye color, hair color, taste preferences, capabilities, talents—is already within her as written in her DNA. The work of creation is done. The work of growth and the adventure of life are just beginning. In many ways, the infant is beginning the most exciting part of life—the stages of growth and discovery. The infant will grow into an adult, but her DNA will not change. The grown woman will not look or act like the infant she used to be, but her DNA is the same.

Are you in this stage today? The work of creation, of God

filling you with His Spirit, has already been accomplished. All that you are and will be is now within you through your new spiritual DNA. It's all right if you still feel the same. More adventure is ahead for you—more mountains to climb, more experiences to share, a deeper relationship with the Lord to develop. God isn't frustrated by your failings; He delights in moving you past them, watching you grow and live according to this new spiritual DNA He's given you. Just as a mother is thrilled when her child learns to do new things, discovers new worlds, and has new adventures, God delights in every step of your growth. He isn't maturing you into someone different any more than a mother is growing her child into someone different. Rather, the goal of your growth is to fully express all the wonders, beauty, and talents already within you.

So when you get frustrated with yourself, and when you're tempted to believe you aren't a new creation, remember that God's very grace is woven into your DNA right along with your new identity in Him. You *are* a new creation who will walk in His grace in new ways every day. You *are* a new creation, and you have a lifetime to discover all the beautiful ways you will express your new identity in Christ.

Lord, sometimes I am discouraged about my progress,
especially when it seems I'm living out the mistakes
and insecurities of the "old" me. Your Word says I am
a new creation. I know Your Word is true even when
I don't feel it. Help me catch a glimpse of the woman
I am because Your love lives within me.

The Desert Years

Moses said to God, "Who am I, that I should go to Pharaoh and bring the Israelites out of Egypt?"

EXODUS 3:11

Although he was a Hebrew, Moses grew up as the privileged adopted son of Pharaoh's daughter. When he was grown, he watched as the Egyptian slave owners mistreated their Hebrew slaves. When he saw an Egyptian beating a Hebrew, Moses murdered the abuser. Realizing he would get caught and punished, Moses fled to Midian for safety. He lived for decades in the desert as a result. And this was the man God chose to lead His people out of Egypt and through the desert to the edge of the Promised Land!

Henri Nouwen wrote, "The great illusion of leadership is to think that man can be led out of the desert by someone who has never been there." How fascinating to consider that Moses' terrible deed and his years of hiding in Midian were used by God to prepare him for leadership.

This same principle holds true for you too. God will transform your mistakes, misjudgments, and sinful acts into stepping-stones of growth that will prepare you for the work He has for you to accomplish. This doesn't mean He condones what you've done, but when you repent and turn to Him, He will redeem your transgressions and use them to help you grow spiritually so you can lead other people into God's peace. You can be a leader who reaches out to the women who believe they are too lost in the desert to be touched by God's grace.

Are you doubtful? Are you echoing Moses' words when he said to God, "Who am I, that I should go to Pharaoh and bring the Israelites out of Egypt?" Moses didn't question God's ability to deliver the people or His good intentions in doing so. Moses only doubted God's choice of leader. I believe this reveals that Moses spent a lot of time in the desert reminding himself of his failings and the ways he'd disappointed people and himself.

Life in the desert had prepared Moses in many ways, but it hadn't healed his wounds of self-loathing. And yet God was intent on using this man to help others. In fact, as we read the life story of Moses and the great deliverance of God's people, Moses never forgot his failings. He never grew prideful or believed God used him because he had somehow earned it. Moses knew he was a flawed man, and his awareness of this made him a compassionate leader capable of enduring the mistakes, rebellion, and flaws of the people he was sent to lead.

Lord, You have chosen me and called me to help lead other women to Your grace. Thank You for being willing to redeem my flaws and foibles, my mistakes and sins, my time wasted in regret and anxiety, and turn them into assets that will help me reach out to people with Your love, compassion, and mercy.

True Elegance

Comfort, comfort my people, says your God.

ISAIAH 40:1

oco Chanel said, "Elegance is not the prerogative of those who have just escaped from adolescence, but of those who have already taken possession of their future." How we dress reflects what we expect from the world, from God, from our future, and from today. We also dress in ways that reveal our mood and self-expression.

When I'm feeling frumpy, I wear subdued clothes that will help me stay in the background. That way when I go to the grocery store I can blend in and not be spotted or approached. When I see someone I know I slink into a different aisle and pretend to focus on a food label to avoid saying hello. Only recently have I realized that this might hamper God's plan to use me in someone else's life.

A friend of mine is always polished when she walks out the door, so she is confident and seldom hesitates to meet and greet people. For a while it seemed like every time Renee went to the grocery store she ran into a woman she knew casually. Renee always stopped and said hello to Amber, engaging her in a brief conversation. I know Amber well, and one day she told me about always running into Renee at the store. Because she knew Renee was a passionate believer, Amber believed seeing her was a sign from God to get her life in order. She thought God was encouraging her to do the right thing and make the right choices by putting Renee in her path.

What Renee didn't know was that Amber was on the verge of making a huge, life-altering choice. She was struggling, fighting temptation, and felt alone in the battle. Because Renee, known for her faith in Christ, stopped every time she saw her and said hello, Amber felt God was reaching out to her with His love, grace, and mercy. Amber was encouraged to persevere in a way that honored God.

There's nothing sinful about wearing sweatpants or not dressing up, but when we use our appearance as an excuse to avoid or shy away from people, we might be interfering with what God has planned to do through us to bless others. We might be missing out on blessing someone else and being blessed! So whether we're dressing for comfort or appearance, let's remember that the people we meet may need us more than we know. Hurting people don't care what we look like; they care how we can encourage them and make them feel better.

The desire to care more for people's hearts than how we're feeling or how we look is the basis for true elegance and lasting beauty.

Lord, help me be a woman of true elegance and lasting beauty, a woman who cares more for the condition of another person's heart than the state of my dress. Whether I'm in sweats or my painting clothes, help me shake off my preoccupation with self to focus on others and make sure they know that I see them, that I am available for them. I want to be Your light and love that will bring them peace and comfort.

Trusting Jesus

You do not have, because you do not ask God.
When you ask, you do not receive, because
you ask with wrong motives, that you may spend
what you get on your pleasures...Humble
yourselves before the Lord, and he will lift you up.

James 4:2-3,10

If the Lord were to ask us one question, I think it might be, "Do you trust Me?" When circumstances are bleak, finances fall apart, our weight creeps up, and our past love marries a woman who looks like a supermodel, Jesus is standing right beside us, whispering, "Do you trust Me?" He stands with us as time and circumstances strip away so many things we thought we needed or wanted and what we once prayed fervently for.

"Do you trust Me?"

When life isn't going our way and when we spend time with God and in His Word, we begin to understand that His plan for our lives, our bodies, and our futures might be quite different than ours. God may not want the same things for us that we think we do. How can we trust God and put our lives into Jesus' hands if we're not sure God desires for us what we do? Does trusting God mean we might have to give up our dreams and desires?

In those moments I have to challenge myself to believe the truth. What is the truth? We haven't asked for too much or for the wrong things. We've asked for too little…and for the wrong reasons. We ask for things to soothe our wounds, but God wants to cure them. We ask for things that distract and make life feel pleasant, but God wants to grab our attention and show us the secret to true joy. We ask for things because we don't want to endure a difficult season of growth, but God wants us to have the riches of maturing into His love and our new identity as His beloved daughters.

God finds such delight in us that it would break His heart to give us cheap gifts. He is a loving Father who wants to lavish true riches on His daughters—riches that cannot be stolen or tarnished with time. God wants us to flourish, growing into His beauty and His love. He wants to bless us so much more than anything we can imagine.

Pray today for what you desire, whether it's a number on the scale or a new habit you want to start. But also give God permission to bless you in ways He chooses. You'll be amazed, pleased, and delighted by the extravagant grace of your Father in heaven as your life unfolds.

Lord, remind me today how much You love me. Help me realize I'm Your beloved daughter. As I share with You my prayer requests and desires, remind me that I can trust You with the answers for each season of my life. Please guide my life in ways that honor You, helps me mature, and leads me into beauty.

Never Enough

Consider how the lilies grow.
They do not labor or spin.
Yet I tell you, not even Solomon in all his splendor
was dressed like one of these.

LUKE 12:27

When we place our confidence in our appearance, we open ourselves to anxiety, fear, and doubt. Our appearance changes every day, just as our weight does. Whether the changes are too small to be seen by the eye or so prominent no one could possibly miss them, the fluctuations are there.

There is one certainty, however. We can place our full confidence in God's ever-present, all-embracing love and forgiveness. And when we do that, an amazing transformation happens. We each become beautiful in unique ways. Beauty radiates from within us. Our faces glow, our eyes twinkle, and people desire to spend time with us. This sparkle that draws others to us is the real definition and power of beauty.

Have you considered God's creativity in this light? Why does He give flowers vivid colors and beautiful scents? Isn't it to attract bees and butterflies and birds, all of which will, in turn, help propagate more life? God uses beauty in the world to draw everyone—and everything—into participating in His love and creation.

God's beauty is within you, and when you place your confidence in Him, you radiate His love outward. People are drawn to you because they want what you have. God allows us to participate in His love and plan to offer salvation to all who will believe in and accept His Son's loving sacrifice. With God's love we become radiant, beautiful women. His love works miracles in our lives and in the world around us.

Lord, Your love within me makes me beautiful. Help me soften my expression and open my hands so I am approachable and will receive others with compassion and thoughtfulness. Please give me the best, most lasting beauty. I long for You.

Banishing Shame

*The eyes of both of them were opened,
and they realized they were naked;
so they sewed fig leaves together and
made coverings for themselves.*

GENESIS 3:7

Adam and Eve ate the forbidden fruit from the tree that held the knowledge of good and evil. After they ate the fruit, their eyes were opened and they realized they were naked. In shame, they constructed the first set of clothes to hide their bodies from each other and from God. I've always approached this story with the understanding that Eve and Adam were only ashamed of being naked. But what if their shame was more than just an awareness of nudity?

The more I contemplate this, the more I believe part of their shame was suddenly realizing they were different from each other. When Adam was first introduced to Eve, he didn't comment on their differences, although he surely was aware of them. Instead he said, "This is now bone of my bones and flesh of my flesh" (Genesis 2:23). He emphasized their unity even while seeing their differences. But when shame entered their lives, their unity was broken. Each was ashamed of the nakedness and the obvious differences. A strange seed was planted in the world that day that carries over into the minds of each one of us. This seed is the belief that we are different and a shameful suspicion that being different is not good. We are embarrassed not just of our nakedness, but also of our bodies and our differences from each other.

Praise God that Jesus sets us free from shame! Women are different from men, and every man and woman is different from every other man and woman, but in Jesus, we find our unity again. We discover our differences are no cause for shame. We can acknowledge them and know we're all beautiful creations made in the image of our heavenly Father.

The serpent of this world—the father of lies, the devil—wants you to stay trapped in that first shame. He wants you to be ashamed of your body and the differences between you and everyone else. But Jesus wants to set you free. He wants you to *celebrate* your design. He wants to banish shame in any form from your life. You are unique, beautiful, and a joy to Him.

> Lord, it's so easy to believe that differences are bad. Shame takes root so quickly, especially when I look at other bodies and see how different mine is. Please help me banish shame from my mind, my heart, and my life. By faith and trust I know that my differences are God-created and God-blessed!

Choosing a Better Way

There is a way that seems right to a man,
but in the end it leads to death.

PROVERBS 14:12

I was at a party celebrating a dear friend's birthday when a woman I'd just met told me about her difficulties in landing good acting roles. She explained that she didn't have the "perfect modern figure" or ideal measurements, so she was often passed over in favor of actors who were thinner and had fewer curves.

She sighed and placed her hand on my arm. "In the past," she said, "women like us would have been painted by the masters." I grinned because I understood. I am a "woman of substance," which is a nice way of saying God was generous with the curves when He created me. I've struggled to accept myself as beautiful and to believe and accept my husband's love and acceptance.

I love what my new friend was reminding me of: In the past, the great master painters really would have glorified bodies like ours. Curvy and plump women were the ideal. When I thumb through my art books, I see that women's bodies have been celebrated throughout history, and in the olden days the artists leaned toward painting women with generous proportions. (Maybe they just needed to fill a really big canvas. I prefer to think we were beautiful to their artistic eyes.) Generously proportioned women showed that their husbands were so well off that getting enough food wasn't a problem and that their wives could be "women of leisure," not having to do physical labor to make ends meet.

God warns us in Proverbs 14:12: "There is a way that seems right to a man, but in the end it leads to death." Did you know that these same words are repeated in Proverbs 16:25? Like any good parent, God often repeats a message when He doesn't want us to miss it. In these verses God is warning us not to trust our perceptions of what is right and not to go down paths He doesn't specifically lead us to. These verses speak to me about obsession and our definition of beauty. As a culture, we have defined beauty in very narrow terms (pun intended). We have set beauty standards by a certain weight, a certain look, and a certain color. We see these images, and they seem right to us. The women who fit the description *are* beautiful. But they aren't the only beautiful women! If we persist in going down the worldly path of one narrow definition of beauty, we will find ourselves surrounded by sorrow, depression, alienation, and death to our spirits.

Please embrace the beauty God has given you. Trust Him to lead you to a life-giving path.

God, today's culture tries to constrict Your artistic diversity, Your creative passion for color, form, and flourish. I know You are pleased with the way You made me. You are delighted in me, and You created me head to toe so I can best fulfill Your specific plans for my life. Give me the courage to love me just as I am, just as You created me.

God Goes Before You

*The LORD himself goes before you and will be
with you; he will never leave you nor forsake you.
Do not be afraid; do not be discouraged.*

DEUTERONOMY 31:8

In war combatants try to inflict horrific damage on the opposing side's soldiers by hiding explosives. After World War II, in fact, unexploded bombs were discovered in the most inconceivable of places: inside bookcases, statues, and gardens. More bombs were found underground, making every step potentially treacherous. One of the most dangerous jobs for soldiers was to "sweep" areas for bombs, uncover them, and disarm them.

Jesus is a "sweeper" for you and me. The bombs Satan sets become little more than duds because our Lord knows how to disarm them. Have you ever seen an explosive that was a dud? Or a firecracker that refused to pop? The fuse gets lit, there is a little fire, a little smoke, and then nothing... nothing...nothing...until you realize it's over. Nothing else is going to happen.

Jesus goes before us into every day. He disarms the traps the devil has laid for us. Jesus provides for our safety in a hostile environment. Today's world, especially its beliefs about beauty, is certainly adversarial. People say cruel things. Loved ones reject and disappoint us because they don't approve of our appearance, bodies, or standards. Magazines and media hound us to conform or die trying. Every day we come across landmines designed to trap us or destroy our peace and trust in God.

Praise God that Jesus walks through and disarms every one of these traps before you step on them. And He did this before you were born! Jesus knows everything you will face today, tomorrow, and next year. He has found and destroyed every bomb. Nothing can destroy your relationship with Him, and nothing can destroy the peace, comfort, and complete acceptance you have in Him.

The enemy's plots to destroy you have collapsed. Your enemy is defeated. You can move forward in confidence and peace knowing Jesus has cleared the way. Whatever you face today—whether it's the scale, the mirror, or your inner critic—know that you are safe. There might be a little smoke, a little fire, but nothing has the power to destroy you. Romans 8:37 says you and I "are more than conquerors through him who loved us."

God, You are so merciful, so wise, and so protective of me. You have seen every one of my days before even one came to be. You know the hurts I've had and the hurts I will experience. You have taken the destructive power out of each of them by placing me within the strong and safe center of Your love. Nothing can destroy me now because I am safe in You.

Riches Without Relationship

There was a man who had two sons.
The younger one said to his father,
"Father, give me my share of the estate."
So he divided his property between them.

LUKE 15:11-12

Are you familiar with the parable of the prodigal son? As the son of a wealthy father, this young man demanded his inheritance while his father was still alive. After receiving the wealth, he runs off and squanders it all on worldly pleasures. Soon the son is empty financially, emotionally, and relationally. Distraught, broke, and broken, he decides to return home even though he's convinced his father will receive him back but expect him to work as a servant. When the father spies him in the distance, however, he runs to him and even throws a welcome home party!

This parable centers around relationships and what people want. The younger son didn't want a close relationship with his father; he wanted the riches his father had so he could live it up and go his own way. Later, when the son realized he would be better off working as a servant in his father's house than continuing as he was, he was shocked to find his father was waiting with open arms. The father obviously valued relationship over wealth.

What would you rather have from God—His riches or a relationship with Him? Would you trade spending time at His feet for a year of answered prayers? I admit there are many days when I want answers to my prayers—His riches—more than I want to focus on my relationship with Him. Some days it seems my relationship with Him is all about a means to a specific end. I want Him to make me rich in every way and forgo the loving discipline and guidance an authentic relationship entails. I get spiritually exhausted and even lazy sometimes. My attitude gets bent out of shape. I get ill-tempered.

Yes, I'm a prodigal daughter at times. I focus on achieving "perfect beauty" and a "perfect figure" more than increasing and deepening my relationship with my heavenly Father. Thankfully He sees me as already perfected through His Son. And He understands my failings and realizes that ultimately my desire is to be with Him and serve Him. When I realize I've strayed from the path He set before me, I pray, I repent, and I ask Him for forgiveness. I run to Him and crave His loving discipline and guidance.

Lord, I so understand the prodigal son. When I am having a prodigal moment, when I am demanding a better body, a better beauty, a better house, a better

life, and so on, help me remember You are my loving Father. And when I make iffy decisions, I know You still love me as I muddle through the consequences and turn to You. Thank You for always being ready to embrace me with open arms.

A Gentle and Quiet Spirit

Your beauty should not come from outward
adornment, such as braided hair and the
wearing of gold jewelry and fine clothes.
Instead, it should be that of your inner self,
the unfading beauty of a gentle and quiet
spirit, which is of great worth in God's sight.

1 PETER 3:3-4

How do you walk when you are carrying something expensive? If you're like me, you walk slowly, are careful with every step, you pay close attention to the people around you, you watch out for any animals or items that might obstruct your path. This is what it means to have a gentle spirit. You are aware of others, and you are aware that you must be careful as you walk through your day because you carry something very valuable.

And what does having a quiet spirit really mean? Women have asked me how a woman can have a quiet spirit and still love and participate in laughter and horseplay. A quiet spirit doesn't mean a quiet mouth or still hands. You can be the life of the party and still have a gentle spirit. A quiet spirit is simply a spirit undisturbed. Picture a pool of water, still and calm. This is your spirit. It's not trembling. It's not throwing out rings and rings of waves like a stone thrown into a lake does. And yet a current flows steadily, bringing in life and energy. A quiet spirit is at rest, at peace in Christ.

And treating others with gentleness is not just about their needs; it's about yours as a woman of beauty. We want to affirm to people that they are of great worth, and we want to behave in a manner consistent with being daughters of the most high God. Gentleness communicates deep respect for God residing within you and the people around you. A quiet spirit is at rest, secure in Christ. This unique beauty invites others to come and sit with us. They long for the peace and tranquility we exhibit, which gives us an opening to share the Good News of the gospel of Jesus.

The unfading beauty of a gentle and quiet spirit doesn't mean we can't be boisterous or full of good-natured fun. It's really about attitude. When we radiate these delightful inner qualities, our appearance is transformed. Frown lines disappear, shoulders relax, smiles broaden, and our eyes sparkle.

Let's show the world how delightful it is to be women of God! To be beautiful in Him.

Lord, You love beauty. In fact, You came up with the concept of beauty. And because You love me, You created me beautiful too. Thank You for wanting the very best for me. I'm at peace and my spirit is gentle and quiet. May others find Your reflection in me delightful so I can point them to Your loving goodness.

Dressing for Our Identity

She is clothed with strength and dignity;
she can laugh at the days to come.

PROVERBS 31:25

*L*et's take a field trip today, shall we? We can do something different…perhaps even exciting. Let's go through your closet. I can't be there in person, but why not ask Jesus to join you? He knows all the clothes in there already so you don't have to worry that He'll disapprove or groan about your taste. He was with you when you purchased the clothes (even if you didn't ask His opinion about them at the time!). Together the two of you can decide if some changes can be made to better reflect His taste, your taste, and perhaps even clean out some clutter.

When you gaze into your closet, are there clothes you are uncomfortable in because of their size, style, or message? Are there clothes that don't fit your body and don't fit who you are in Christ—a woman of quiet strength and dignity? I've heard it said that we should dress for the job or position we want. Instead, I believe we should dress for the identity we've been given in Christ Jesus. We are His beautiful women, daughters of the King of kings, chosen before the creation of the world, and filled with His hope, love, and joy. We are women who look forward to the future and eternity because of whose love resides within us.

Does viewing your clothing through this lens seem a bit over the top? I understand, but I also realized that I needed to do some clothes cleaning of my own. I've taken several bags of clothes to a local charity. I had tight skirts that revealed too much of my obvious curves, shirts that resembled surplus tents, and belts that went out of style years ago.

I decided to keep only those clothes that projected my true identity in Christ, that reminded me that I'm a strong, dignified, loving woman with a vital message to share that offers love to a hurting world. I want to make sure my body doesn't court the envy of others or stir up lust. I want my dress to not overwhelm my message, meaning my clothes won't encourage critical judgments and let me fade into the background.

You and I are women of power in Christ. We represent our incredible heavenly Father. We are loved enough, provided for enough, and given strength enough to reach out to others with servant hearts, declining to draw attention to ourselves so we can point people to our Savior and Lord.

God, Your Word is filled with such inspiring, revolutionary truths! In You I am a woman of strength and dignity. What a blessing. And what a call to action! Please be with me today as I dress, go out, meet with people, and represent You. Guide my decisions so my life and presence will reflect the incredible beauty of You.

Gaps in the Sidewalk

Many are the plans in a man's heart,
but it is the LORD's purpose that prevails.

PROVERBS 19:21

While walking down a concrete sidewalk I noticed a tiny green plant shoving its way up through a small gap. I was startled, and then I considered the implications. How bold, how daring this little dandelion was! So many people had been involved in creating this solid walking structure. Plans had been drawn up, budgets had been approved, materials were purchased and shipped, workers hired, and inspections completed. Now, in a relatively short time, a tiny plant had located a tiny flaw and used it to reclaim the land for plant life.

I smiled at this tiny green plant because it reminded me that nothing mankind does on this earth is guaranteed to turn out perfectly or last forever. There's always a gap somewhere. And whenever a gap appears, something moves in and fills it up. Beauty, like this audacious dandelion, appears in the strangest of places.

I work and write in the beauty industry, so this is a great reminder. Fashion designers create elaborate, expensive fashions but a young girl can turn the entire industry on its ear by starting an unexpected, new trend. We're told by experts that diet plans based on extensive research will melt the most stubborn pounds so that we can lose weight and rediscover the wonders of life. But seldom are they easy or successful over the long term.

Human plans can't guarantee perfection or even satisfaction! We can't be sure if our plans will even last past this hour. What we can know is that life—creative, glorious, beautiful, resilient life—is all around us, filling in the gaps we leave, bringing beauty where we least expect it.

Look around as you go through your day and discover beauty. Find the places where, despite our efforts to contain and command life, God finds the gaps and fills them with unexpected glimpses of His majesty and creativity.

Lord, when I fail a diet, abandon a skin-care regimen that was carefully planned, or prefer sweats to expensive clothes, I am tempted to beat myself up emotionally. I think I'm a failure because I have found yet another area where my plans have fallen short. Yet You work miracles in those gaps. When I am tempted to despair, remind me today that my failings are openings for You to surprise .

Do We Really Want Perfection?

Delight yourself in the LORD and he
will give you the desires of your heart.

PSALM 37:4

My grandmother was put into a nursing home. Knowing she is suffering, knowing our time together is coming to a temporary goodbye, knowing that life inevitably ends, fills me with sadness. When the nurses and staff go into my grandmother's room, I wonder who they see. Do they see an old woman, frail and helpless? Or do they see the woman I know to be lavishly beautiful with a laugh that covers several octaves if a joke is told just right?

Grandmother has always been a physically beautiful woman, even into her eighties, and yet she is known for her loving heart and spirit. I can call Grandmom anytime and tell her anything, and she immediately prays for me and reminds me of God's wisdom found in His Word. She has unlimited faith, a joy for life, and a deep love for family and friends. We gravitate to her because of what's inside. We acknowledge her beauty, but we value her spirit.

Through my grandmom's outer and inner beauty I've learned that even for physically beautiful women—the women who seem to have every physical blessing a supermodel could want—the most powerful and substantial glory is in the spirit. My grandmother might have turned heads in her heyday, but she didn't want onlookers to focus on her like rubber-neckers focus on victims at an accident. She wanted love. She wanted to give love. She wanted to show love. Her joyful, kind spirit and constant delight in God's Word enabled her to live abundantly. Because she delighted in the Lord, He gave her the desires of her heart.

A perfect face and a perfect body never has made a woman happy in the long run. In fact, perfection—or the ideal of perfection—has made many women miserable. The hardest battle we may ever face regarding our appearance is the decision to stop pursuing perfection, to acknowledge that it cannot bring us what we want. We don't want perfect beauty, we want perfect lives. We want to be loved completely and unconditionally. We want to be filled and content. We want to be safe and honored.

Beauty can't fill those needs, but God can and will. He can provide what you're looking for today—and He wants to! Before you double your efforts to lose weight, tame your hair, conquer skin problems, or take drastic measures to attain the beauty you think will make you happy, why not consider addressing the real reason this battle seems so important to you? If you're looking for emotional payoffs or relational peace, you won't find it in any physical attribute. Even when there is worldly beauty, those qualities eventually fade and decay.

For lasting beauty and joy seek the love, acceptance, security, honor, and joy that God longs to bring to you in abundance. He will bless you and ease your burdens. He longs to carry you in His arms to a place of rest and renewal in His love. Turn to Him. Ask Him to fill you with His love and guide you in His perfect and beautiful ways.

Lord, help me grasp the truth that joy and peace reside in You and come only through You. Let this sink into the very marrow of my bones. No matter what I do in my own human ability, I will always hunger for more because what I'm really seeking is You. Heal my wounds and make me whole in You. Grant me deeper faith, richer peace, and a stronger appreciation for the true beauty of love as expressed through Jesus Christ.

Answering Insecurity

Do nothing out of selfish ambition or
vain conceit, but in humility consider
others better than yourselves.

PHILIPPIANS 2:3

had a lunch date with a beautiful celebrity model who wanted to develop a book. I was uneasy off and on for days before the luncheon. What would I wear? Would she think I was too fat, too old, too frumpish? I was so grateful that when those thoughts came I could focus on the truth that my appearance wasn't as important as Christ's love in my spirit, attitude, and skills. Every woman wants to be loved, accepted, and approved of—including celebrities. What mattered most was how my new friend felt after our time together. Would *she* feel accepted or judged? Would *she* feel loved or criticized?

The Bible gives us a startling technique for ending debilitating insecurities: consider others better than yourself. While self-help gurus might tell us that we have to love ourselves more if we are to break free from insecurity, God asks us to love ourselves less and others more. We're to stop worrying about whether others will love us and, instead, focus on how best to love others. This advice frees us from insecurity because it eliminates self-centeredness.

When I am most insecure, I am most self-centered. To break free of insecurity, I need to retrain my thoughts to concentrate on making others feel comfortable, accepted, beautiful, and appreciated. I need to develop the habit of focusing on the other person as soon as the worry or insecurity makes itself known. In loving others, I forget myself.

What happened with my lunch date? The model was every bit as gorgeous as I remembered from her photographs. She had a perfect figure and graceful manners. Throughout the lunch I kept reminding myself to focus on what she was sharing, what her needs were, and how I could help her. As we paid the bill and walked into the sunshine of a crowded city street, peace swept over me. I felt good in my own skin. I was content with myself just as I was. I admit this was a curious feeling! And I knew I had made a friend because the meeting went so well that both of us relaxed and connected. We found a hundred things in common and a hundred things to laugh at. And, surprise! She confessed she'd been nervous before lunch. I laughed at the irony of God hearing both of our prayers in the days before the luncheon, each of us praying to make a good impression and win the approval of the other. All the while, God wanted us to freely give approval to one another so that we'd discover how much we needed each other. We were both daughters of the divine God.

God, insecurities tempt me to focus on myself. I can become obsessed with everything I am not and everything I wish I were. When I am feeling insecure, please remind me of Your secret to freedom: to consider others better than myself. Teach me how to zero in on serving others, offering to help where I can and giving words of encouragement.

Pay Attention to the Pain

Listen and hear my voice;
pay attention and hear what I say.

ISAIAH 28:23

love being active. "Pedal till you puke" was a mantra of my triathlon training, and I embraced all the other tough-girl sayings too, including: "If you're not in pain, you're not working hard enough." So when my left ankle began getting sore after races or runs, I ignored it. *Pain is to be ignored,* I told myself. *Pain is a sign I am working hard.*

After I ran a half-marathon with one of my best girlfriends, my left ankle was on fire. Still I ignored it. I didn't have time to go to the doctor, especially for something as insignificant as a sore joint. After all, I had three young kids at home and a busy life to lead. Then a strange thing began happening. I would be standing up, washing dishes or walking down the hall, and my left side would give way. I wasn't dizzy or sick, and I couldn't figure out why I kept losing my balance. Finally the foot pain began waking me up at night, and I made a spectacle of myself falling one too many times to ignore the problem anymore.

I went to the doctor, and after the exam the ankle specialist shook his head. "You have a serious injury to your tendons. You need surgery. And you might never run again."

At that moment I would have given almost anything to go back and experience that first twinge of pain so I could do something about it this time around. If I had paid attention to the pain, I could have more easily healed the problem and continued to lead the life I loved. This lesson taught me the truth about pain: Pain signals a problem, and some problems will not go away without intervention. Some problems grow bigger and nastier if left unattended.

Needless to say, now I pay attention to my aches and pains. And I've even learned that even my spirit sends me pain signals when something needs attention. Every time I feel a twinge of anxiety about my beauty, appearance, or weight, my spirit is sending me a pain signal. Working together with the Holy Spirit, my spirit wants to communicate with my mind and heart to show me where my faith and my beliefs have slipped onto separate paths, no longer working together. These twinges of anxiety aren't really over my appearance, but rather are warning bells that my beliefs do not line up with God's truth. They are alerting me to a wound, to damage being done, to a tender spot that needs attention and healing.

Can you relate? Why not take a moment as soon as you feel a hint of pain and ask God to show you what isn't quite right. Listen to God speak to you and let the healing happen. He can heal you in the middle of a grocery store, while you're in line at the bank, or as you're doing laundry at midnight. You don't have to travel to a monastery for a silent retreat or take a pilgrimage to the Holy Land to find God. God has already found you! He will work wherever you are, whenever you call out to Him.

Lord, when I am tempted to sweep my anxieties under the rug and ignore them, please slow me down. Remind me to listen for Your voice and see what I need to change, whether it be my thought life, my words, or my focus. Thank You for bringing my wounds to my attention so I can address them by turning to You for healing.

Notes

"Feeling Beautiful"

1. Gale Berkowitz, "UCLA Study on Friendship Among Women," www .anapsid.org/cnd/gender/tendfend.html, quoting Harvard Nurses' Study, accessed August 2010.

"Beauty in Healing"

2. Shaun Dreisback, "Exclusive Body-Image Survey," http://www.glamour .com/health-fitness/2009/03/women-tell-their-body-confidence -secrets, accessed August 2010.

"Miracles Still Happen"

3. See Gregory Fung and Christopher Fung, "What Do Prayer Studies Prove?" http://www.christianitytoday.com/ct/2009/may/27.43.html, accessed August 2010.

"Accepting Ourselves"

4. Nancy Etcoff, et al., "The Real Truth About Beauty: A Global Report," http://www.campaignforrealbeauty.com/uploadedfiles/dove_white _paper_final.pdf, accessed August 2010.

"Honoring God and Others"

5. "What Is Human Trafficking"? www.polarisproject.org, accessed August 2010.

"God's Divine Power"

6. Lisa Rapport, "Designer Vagina Surgery Is a $5,500 Risk, Doctors Say" (Update2), August 31, 2007, www.bloomberg.com, accessed August 2010.

Ginger Garrett

Ginger is the critically acclaimed author of *Chosen: The Lost Diaries of Queen Esther*, which was recognized as one of the top five novels of 2006 by the ECPA, and *Wolves Among Us*. An expert in ancient women's history, Ginger creates novels and nonfiction resources that explore the lives of historical women.

Beauty Secrets of the Bible was based on the research that began in her work on *Chosen*. It explores the connections between beauty and spirituality, offering women both historical insights and scientific proofs that reveal powerful, natural beauty secrets.

A frequent radio guest on stations across the country, including NPR and Billy Graham's *The Hour of Decision*, Ginger is also a popular television guest. Her appearances include *Fox News*, *The Harvest Show*, *Friends & Neighbors*, and *Babbie's House*.

A graduate of Southern Methodist University with a degree in theatre, Ginger is passionate about creating art from history.